Pase el Examen de Ciudadanía Americana

☆ Pass the U.S. Citizenship Exam ☆

Pase el Examen de Ciudadanía Americana

Pass the U.S. Citizenship Exam

MARY MASI

Translated by
Héctor A. Canonge

LEARNINGEXPRESS

NEW YORK

Library of Congress Catalog-in-Publication Data:

Masi, Mari.
   [Pass the U.S. citizenship exam. Spanish]
   Pase el examen de ciudadanía americana / Mary Masi; translated by Héctor A. Canonge.
      p.cm.
   "Portions of this guide have been adapted from "Citizenship", provided by the
Minnesota Literacy Council, additional matereal was adapted from "Study guide to
Prepare for new written citizenship examination: A guide for beginner level ESL
student" provided by Catholic Charities Immigration and Refugee Services of
Harrisburg, Pa."—Publisher's info.
     ISBN 1-57685-394-2
   1. Citizenship—United States—Examinations—Study guides. I. Canonge, Héctor A. II.
Title

2001038970

LearningExpress wishes to thank the following organizations for their contributions
to this book:
The Minnesota Literacy Council; St. Paul, Minnesota
Catholic Charities Immigration and Refugee Services; Harrisburg, Pennsylvania
McDonaugh Organization Organization with Respect and Equality for People
   (MORE); St. Paul, Minnesota

Portions of this guide have been adapted from *Citizenship*, provided by the
Minnesota Literacy Council ©1997. Additional material was adapted from *Study
Guide to Prepare for New Written Citizenship Examination: A Guide for Beginner
Level ESL Students*, provided by Catholic Charities Immigration and Refugee
Services of Harrisburg, Pennsylvania.

ISBN 1-57685-394-2

For more information or to place an order, contact LearningExpress at:
900 Broadway
Suite 604
New York, NY 10003

Or visit us at:
   www.learnatest.com

Un anuncio importante para aquellos lectores que usen la biblioteca

Si has prestado este libro de tu escuela o la biblioteca pública, por favor no escribas en el. En lugar de hacer eso, usa una hoja de papel aparte para escribir tus respuestas y para que así otros lectores puedan usar el material. Gracias por tu ayuda y por tener consideración con otros lectores.

MATERIAL ACTUALIZADO

A pesar de que puedes tener varios niveles de conocimiento de la historia y educación cívica de los Estados Unidos, en este libro encontrarás el material que te ayude a pasar el examen de ciudadanía. Recuerda que muchas veces la información puede ser vieja; como por ejemplo los pasos difíciles para la solicitud o el nombre del actual presidente estadounidense.

ACERCA DE LA INFORMACIÓN EN ESTE LIBRO

Antes de su publicación, tratamos de verificar la información presentada en nuestro libro. Es siempre una buena idea chequear dos veces con el Servicio de Imigración y Naturalización, la solicitud y los procedimientos de prueba, ya que esta información puede cambiar de tiempo en tiempo. Este libro no ofrece consejo legal. Para ayuda con tu situación de inmigración consulta con un abogado.

CONTENIDO

CÓMO USAR
ESTE LIBRO

Este libro te ayudará a pasar el examen de ciudadanía estadounidense como también te mostrará los pasos a seguir para llegar a ser ciudadano. Atención, que este libro no provee consejos legales. Consulta con tu abogado para asuntos legales de inmigración. Puedes estudiar este libro por tu propia cuenta, con un compañero(a) de estudio, o en una clase formal.

LO QUE ENCONTRARÁS EN ESTE LIBRO

Capítulo 1 muestra los beneficios y los pormenores potenciales de llegar a ser ciudadano estadounidense. Tienes que saber porqué quieres llegar a ser ciudadano ya que el Servicio de Inmigración, INS, te pedirá explicar tus razones. **Capítulo 2** explica lo que tienes que hacer para convertirte en ciudadano. Recuerda que las leyes de naturalización pueden cambiar. Pregunta a tu abogado o a alguien del Servicio de Inmigración y Naturalización, INS, sobre la información más reciente. **Capítulo 3** muestra que oficina regional del INS tienes que contactar para obtener más información o para enviar la solicitud completa del formulario N-400.

Capítulo 4 es el más largo del libro. Tiene 23 lecciones sobre la historia de los Estados Unidos y del gobierno estadounidense. Cada lección comienza con una lista de palabras que pueden ser nuevas para tí, luego podrás encontrar información sobre algún tema en particular. Esta información aparecerá en inglés como también en español. La próxima página de cada lección comienza con una lista de preguntas del INS que tienes que memorizar. Una vez que hayas memorizado las preguntas y respuestas, y de que hayas estudiado la información al comienzo de la lección, haz los ejercicios que siguen para asegurarte que recuerdas la información. Las respuestas a estos ejercicios puedes encontrarlas en la última página de cada lección. Trata de no mirar las respuestas hasta que hayas tratado de responder por tu propia cuenta todas las preguntas.

Cada lección te dará la práctica de dictado que necesitas. Dictado es cuando el agente del INS dice una oración en voz alta y tú tienes que escribirla. En cada lección también podras practicar la entrevista; primero practicarás leyendo ejemplos de preguntas y respuestas de entrevista, y luego practicarás respondiendo con tus propias respuestas. Una vez más, ambas partes de dictado y entrevista del examen se llevan a cabo en inglés.

En cada lección existen incorporados seis exámenes de preparación. A medida que vayas estudiando las lecciones, toma cada uno de los exámenes de preparación. Las respuestas las puedes encontrar en la última página del examen de preparación.

Capítulo 5 es una lista de todas las palabras de las 23 lecciones del Capítulo 4 que quizás requieran tu atención. Estas palabras se encuentran en orden alfabético (de la A–Z) y en inglés. Debajo de cada palabra y de su definición en inglés, aparece la palabra y su respectiva definición en español. Esto te puede servir como un diccionario si es que en algún momento tienes problemas con algunas de las palabras que encuentres mientras te preparas para el examen.

Capítulo 6 es una lista ordenada por temas de 100 preguntas y respuestas oficiales del INS. Todas estas preguntas y respuestas son del Capítulo 4. Lee el capítulo 6 cuando quieras revisar las preguntas sobre la historia y el gobierno de los Estados Unidos; cubre las respuestas para que así puedas evaluarte a tí mismo. Seguidamente, puedes comprobar si has contestado las preguntas correctamente.

Capítulo 7 te mostrará muchos ejemplos de preguntas y respuestas del formulario N-400 "Solicitud para Naturalización." Estas son preguntas que una persona del INS puede preguntarte el día de tu entrevista. Algunas preguntas pueden pedir la misma información pero de diferente manera. Piensa como podrías responder cada pregunta antes de ver la posible respuesta. Todas estas preguntas y respuestas de ejemplo corresponden al capítulo 4.

Capítulo 8 te da en una lista todas las oraciones de dictado del Capítulo 4. Puedes practicar escribiendo cada oración en el espacio de la página opuesta.

Apéndice A al final del libro, es una copia del formulario N-400 "Solicitud para Naturalización" para que puedas practicar como llenar la información necesaria.

Pase el Examen de Ciudadanía Americana

☆ **Pass the U.S. Citizenship Exam** ☆

CAPÍTULO 1

¿Quieres Ser Ciudadano?

Hay muchas razonas por las cuales muchas personas quieren llegar a ser ciudadanos estadounidenses. Como también hay otras tantas por las que muchas se niegan a hacerlo. Piensa porqué quieres llegar a ser un ciudadano de los Estados Unidos. A través de este libro, los siguientes términos se usaran indistintamente América, U.S., y Estados Unidos. Un ciudadano "americano" es lo mismo que un ciudadano estadounidense.

RAZONES PARA SER CIUDADANO

Estos son algunos de los beneficios de convertirse en ciudadano estadounidense. Ponte a pensar qué significan las cosas de la lista que sigue a continuación. Pon una marca al lado de las cosas por las que tú quieres convertirte en ciudadano "americano."

_____ Tienes el derecho a votar en las elecciones.

_____ Puedes postular a un cargo público.

_____ Puedes solicitar empleo con el gobierno.

_____ Puedes solicitar que tus familiares inmediatos vengan a los Estados Unidos.

_____ Miembros de tu familia pueden obtener venir a los Estados Unidos rápidamente.

_____ Más miembros de tu familia pueden ser capaces de venir a los Estados Unidos.

_____ Tus hijos solteros pueden solicitar la ciudadanía.

_____ Puedes obtener beneficios del seguro social incluso si vives en otro país.

_____ Puedes vivir fuera de los Estados Unidos sin miedo a perder tu ciudadanía.

_____ Puedes viajar con un pasaporte "americano."

_____ Puedes reingresar a los Estados Unidos más fácilmente.

_____ No tienes que renovar tu tarjeta de residencia, _Green Card_.

_____ No tienes que notificar en caso de un cambio de domicilio.

_____ No vas a ser deportado.

_____ Obtienes más beneficios del gobierno.

_____ No te tienes que preocupar por las nuevas leyes migratorias.

✪ ✪ ✪

ALGUNAS DE LAS RESPONSABILIDADES DE UN CIUDADANO

El juramento de afiliación que vas a tomar para llegar a ser ciudadano cubre solamente algunas de las responsabilidades de un ciudadano estadounidense. Algunas de las otras responsabilidades incluyen:

- ▶ **Participación en el proceso político por medio de la registración para votar y votar en las elecciones.**
- ▶ **Servicio de jurado.**
- ▶ **Mostrar tolerancia hacia las diferentes opiniones, culturas, religiones, y grupos étnicos que se encuentran en los Estados Unidos.**

✪ ✪ ✪

RAZONES PARA NO CONVERTIRSE EN CIUDADANO

_____ Tienes que tomar un juramento de obediencia a los Estados Unidos.

_____ Quizás tengas que darle la espalda a tu país natal.

_____ Puede que tengas que negarte a ayudar a tu país natal.

_____ Puedes perder tu ciudadanía en tu país de origen.

_____ Puedes perder tus propiedades y posesiones en tu país de origen.

_____ Puedes perder el poder de votación en tu país de origen.

_____ Tienes que pasar un corto examen sobre la historia y el gobierno de los Estados Unidos.

_____ Puedes ser deportado si es que mientes en tu solicitud de ciudadanía.

_____ La ciudadanía se te puede negar si has mentido para obtener tu residencia permanente en los Estados Unidos.

Ahora, observa cuantas opciones has marcado. ¿Existen más en la primera lista? Entonces quieres llegar a ser ciudadano de los Estados Unidos. ¿Existen más marcas en la segunda lista? Entonces necesitas saber si puedes obtener doble nacionalidad.

Para mucha gente, las razones para convertirse en ciudadano americano son más grandes que las razones para no hacerlo. Piensa, porqué quieres llegar a ser ciudadano "americano." Puede que necesites responder a esta misma pregunta en tu entrevista con el INS:

✪ · ✪ · ✪

¿Porqué quieres convertirte en ciudadano "americano."
Why do you want to become a United States citizen?

✪ · ✪ · ✪

CAPÍTULO 2

El Proceso Para Convertirse en Ciudadano

Este capítulo te demostrará cómo llegar a ser ciudadano estadounidense. Hay muchos pasos a seguir. Puede tomarte unos cuantos meses para completar todas las etapas. Lee este capítulo cuidadosamente, para que no cometas el error de saltar algún paso.

¿Estás listo?

Encierra en un círculo **Si** o **No**. Si puedes contestar que **Si** a todas las preguntas, entonces quiere decir que estás listo para solicitar la ciudadanía "americana."

Si   No   ¿Tienes por lo menos 18 años de edad?

Si   No   ¿Has sido residente legal y permanente de los Estados Unidos por ya sea cinco (5) años, o tres (3) años si has estado casado(a) por tres años con alguien que es ciudadano(a) por lo menos por tres años?

Si   No   ¿Has estado físicamente presente en los Estados Unidos por lo menos 2 años y medio (2 ½), o medio (½) año si estás casado(a) con un(a) ciudadana(o) de los Estados Unidos.

Si   No   ¿Has vivido en tu mismo estado o distrito por lo menos tres (3) meses?

Si   No   ¿Estás dispuesto(a) a jurar obediencia a los Estados Unidos?

Si   No   ¿Tienes un buen carácter moral?

Si   No   ¿Puedes leer, escribir, y hablar un inglés básico?

Si   No   ¿Tienes conocimiento de la historia y el gobierno de los Estados Unidos?

Si has encerrado en un círculo **Si** a todas las preguntas anteriores, estás listo para solicitar la ciudadanía "americana." Si respondió **No** a algunas de las preguntas anteriores, pregunte a un especialista de inmigración si es que califica para la ciudadanía. Hay muchas razones para responder **No,** que no le impiden solicitar su ciudadanía.

El formulario N-400 hace unas cuantas preguntas sobre asuntos criminales y tu pasado criminal. Siempre debes de contestar a estas preguntas de una forma honesta y clara. Si encuentran que has mentido en tu solicitud, tu petición por ciudadanía será negada, incluso si el delito no es aquel que impida que te hagas ciudadano. Siempre dí la verdad, tanto en el solicitud como en la entrevista.

LA SOLICITUD

Necesitas enviar una solicitud llamada N-400 *"Application for Naturalization"* al Servicio de Inmigración y Naturalización, INS. (NOTA: Puedes llenar tu solicitud N-400 3 meses antes de haber cumplido tus 5 años como residente permanente). Tambien tiene que enviar dos fotos de usted adjunto con un cheque (o un giro de *money order* de un banco estadounidense) por la solicitud, y un cargo de huellas digitales (cuando este libro es estaba imprimiendo, el precio de la solicitud era de $225.00 más el precio de las huellas digitales de $25.00). Estos costos pueden ser pagados en un solo cheque (total de $250.00). Endorse el cheque a nombre del *Immigration and Naturalization Services.*

ENVIA ESTO AL INS:

- ▶ **Formulario N-400 (saca una copia para tí antes de enviar la solicitud original por correo)**
- ▶ **Dos fotos tamaño pasaporte**
- ▶ **Estas fotografías tienen que ser montadas en un papel delgado, de fondo blanco, y con una vista de $\frac{3}{4}$ del lado lateral de tu cara.**
- ▶ **Las fotos tienen que haber sido tomadas en un lapso de 30 días antes de ser enviadas al INS.**

   Con un lápiz tienes que escribir tu nombre completo y tu número de residente permanente en la parte trasera de tus fotos. Esto no es un requisito, pero es sugerido en caso de que sus fotos sean separadas de su solicitud.
- ▶ **Un cheque (o un *money order* de un banco estadounidense) por $250.00**

   Puedes obtener el formulario de solicitud N-400 de una oficina del INS que esté cercano. Ve la lista del Capítulo 3 para información sobre las oficinas del INS. Después puedes tomar uno de los siguientes pasos.
- ▶ **Escribirles una carta solicitando el formulario.**
- ▶ **Ir a la oficina y recogerlo personalmente.**
- ▶ **Llamarles por teléfono y pedirles que envien el formulario.**
- ▶ **Visita www.ins.usdoj.gov/graphics/formsfee/forms/n-400.htm**

✪ ✪ ✪

También puedes obtener el formulario de solicitud N-400 llamando al teléfono 1-800-870-3676. Di la verdad cuando llenes el formulario de solicitud. Pide ayuda si la requieres. Ve el Capítulo 3 para información sobre dónde obtener esta clase de ayuda.

HUELLAS DIGITALES

No envies una carta o tarjeta con tus huellas digitales junto con la solicitud. Después de que el INS reciba tu solicitud, ellos te enviarán una carta con la información del lugar más cercano a tu residencia, y designado por el INS donde te puedes tomar las huellas digitales. Lee las instrucciones de la carta. El día de tu cita, lleva contigo la carta, tu tarjeta de residencia permanente, y otra forma de identificación personal con fotografía (licencia de conducir, pasaporte) a este lugar de huellas digitales designado por el INS. Tus huellas digitales son enviadas al FBI para así poder revisar datos sobre tu pasado criminal. Si tienes mas de 75 años de edad a la hora de hacer esta solicitud, no requieres que te tomen las huellas digitales.

ESTUDIAR

Lee y estudia este libro y cualquier otro material que te ayude a comprender la historia y el gobierno de los Estados Unidos. Necesitas saber el material incluido en este libro. Quizás sea necesario que tomes una clase que indique cómo pasar el examen de ciudadanía "americana."

TOMA UNA PRUEBA

El INS va a necesitar evaluar tu inglés y tu conocimiento del gobierno y la cívica estadounidense. Tienes que probar que puedes leer, escribir, y hablar un inglés básico. Para demostrar que puedes escribir inglés, necesitas escribir oraciones que te dicten.

Durante tu entrevista, el INS te dará un examen acerca de la historia de los Estados Unidos y su gobierno. Te harán preguntas en inglés y tienes que responderlas en voz alta y también en inglés. En algunos casos, puede que te dejen tomar un examen escrito. Para pasar el examen, tienes que responder correctamente un 70% de las preguntas. Puede que te den los resultados de tu examen inmediatamente o aproximadamente dentro de dos meses te enviarán por correo los resultados del mismo. Si no le fue bien en el examen de inglés y en el de cívica, el estado de su solicitud será marcado como "*continued*" (continuado). Esto significa que le preguntarán que haga una segunda respuesta, generalmente dentro de 60 a 90 días. En algunos casos, si no pasas el examen de cívica o inglés pueden negarte la ciudadanía. Puedes hacer una solicitud inmediatamente después, pero tendrás que empezar el proceso de solicitud nuevamente, y tendrás que esperar unos cuantos meses para obtener una nueva entrevista.

✪ ✪ ✪

Si tienes más de cincuenta (50) años y has vivido como residente permanente y legal en los Estados Unidos por veinte (20) años, no tienes

que tomar el examen de inglés. **Puedes tomar el examen de cívica en español.**

▶ **Si tienes más de 55 años y has vivido como residente permanente y legal en los Estados Unidos por 15 años, no tienes que tomar el examen de inglés. Puedes tomar el examen de cívica en español.**

▶ **Si tienes más de 65 años y vivido como residente permanente y legal en los Estados Unidos por 20 años, no tienes que tomar el examen de inglés y puedes tomar una versión más fácil del examen de cívica en español.**

LA ENTREVISTA

Después de que hayas llenado la solicitud, recibirás una carta que especifica la fecha de tu entrevista. No te asombres si tu cita está de aquí a 10 ó 12 meses. Esta notificación puede incluir una petición de documentos adicionales que tienes que llevar en el día de tu entrevista. Si tienes que cambiar la fecha de tu entrevista, contacta tu correspondiente oficina del INS y explícales las razones para cambiar la fecha. No te olvides que puede tomar unos cuantos meses para cambiar la fecha de entrevista. En la entrevista, tienes que tomar un juramento y prometer que vas a decir la verdad. Te harán preguntas de tu formulario de solicitud N-400. También te harán preguntas personales, sobre tus hijos, tu trabajo, y tu vida personal. Tienes que contestar a estas preguntas en inglés. Si tienes un problema físico, mental, o invalidez, tú puedes ser eximido de tomar la parte de inglés y cívica del examen. (NOTA: En la ceremonia de juramento, tienes que estar dispuesto y preparado a tomar juramento de afiliación con los Estados Unidos. Si no puedes entender o tomar el juramento debido a un desahucio, no podrás ser elegible para obtener la ciudadanía.)

Asegúrate que cada vez que cambies de dirección notifiques al INS. Sólo te enviarán una carta notificándote la fecha de tu entrevista. Si tú pierdes esa cita sin haber contactado al INS, tu caso será "*administratively closed*" (terminado administrativamente), y necesitarás re-abrirlo.

★ ★ ★

JURAMENTO EN LA CEREMONIA

Si pasas el examen y la entrevista, recibirás una carta en más o menos dos meses. La carta te dirá la fecha y la hora de la ceremonia de tu juramento. En la ceremonia, tomarás un juramento de obediencia *Oath of Allegiance* (diciendo que eres leal a los Estados Unidos) y cambiarás tu tarjeta de Residencia Permanente por un certificado de ciudadanía de los Estados Unidos. Después de esta ceremonia serás un ciudadano americano.

★ ★ ★

No es sino hasta que tomes tu juramento que te convierte en ciudadano estadounidense. A continuación está el juramento. Abajo encontrarás una traducción general (no palabra por palabra) de ese juramento.

★ ★ ★

★ ★ ★

JURAMENTO DE AFILIACIÓN

Yo aquí declaro, bajo juramento,

Que yo absolutamente, y enteramente renuncio y rechazo toda afiliación y fidelidad a cualquier príncipe, potentado, nación o reino estranjero de quien o de cual yo, antes de hoy, he sido súbdito o ciudadano;

Que voy a apoyar y defender la Constitución y las leyes de los Estados Unidos de

America en contra de todo enemigo, ya sea este foráneo o doméstico;

Que yo voy a cargar la Buena fe y afiliación al mismo;

Que yo voy a cargar armas a favor de los Estados Unidos, cuando la ley lo requiera;

Que yo voy a hacer servicio militar en tiempo en las Fuerzas Armadas de los Estados Unidos cuando la ley lo requiera.

Que voy a desempeñar trabajos de importancia nacional bajo la dirección civil cuando la ley así lo requiera; y

Que tomo esta obligación libremente, sin ninguna reservación mental o propósito de evasion; Entonces

Que Dios me ayude

CAPÍTULO 3

Cómo Obtener Ayuda

Para llegar a ser ciudadano estadounidense puedes encontrar ayuda en muchos lugares. Este capítulo incluye información de contactos en las cuatro regiones del Servicio de Inmigración y Naturalización, INS, para que puedas encontrar una en el área donde vives.

INFORMACIÓN DE LAS OFICINAS DEL INS

Esta es una lista de donde puedes enviar tu formulario de solicitud N-400 "*Application for Naturalization*" completa. Hay cuatro oficinas regionales del INS. Busca tu estado y envia tu solicitud a la dirección que aparece debajo del mismo. También puedes contactar la oficina del INS para más información sobre el proceso de naturalización.

NORTE

Si vives en uno de estos estados:

Alaska	Michigan	Oregon
Colorado	Minnesota	South Dakota
Idaho	Missouri	Utah

Illinois	Montana	Washington
Indiana	Nebraska	Wisconsin
Iowa	North Dakota	Wyoming
Kansas	Ohio	

Envia el formulario de solicitud N-400 completado a esta dirección:
United States Immigration and Naturalization Service
Nebraska Service Center
P.O. Box 87400
Lincoln, NE 68501-7400
402-437-5218

OESTE

Si vives en uno de estos estados u otras áreas:

Arizona
California
Commonwealth of the Northern Mariana Islands
Hawaii
Nevada
Territory of Guam

Envia el formulario de solicitud N-400 completado a esta dirección:

United States Immigration and Naturalization Service
California Service Center
Attention N-400 Unit
P.O. Box 10400
Laguna Niguel, CA 92607-0400
949-360-2769

SUD

Si vives en uno de estos estados:

Alabama	Louisiana	South Carolina
Arkansas	Mississippi	Tennessee
Florida	New Mexico	Texas

Georgia   North Carolina
Kentucky   Oklahoma

Envia el formulario de solicitud N-400 completado a esta dirección:
United States Immigration and Naturalization Service
Texas Service Center
Attention N-400 Unit
P.O. Box 851204
Mesquite, TX 75185-1204
214-381-1423

ESTE

Si vives en uno de estos estados u otras áreas

Commonwealth of Puerto Rico	New Hampshire	Vermont
Connecticut	New Jersey	Virginia
Delaware	New York	Washington, DC
Maine	Pennsylvania	West Virginia
Maryland	Rhode Island	
Massachusetts	U.S. Virgin Islands	

Envia el formulario de solicitud N-400 completado a esta dirección:
United States Immigration and Naturalization Service
Vermont Service Center
Attention N-400 Unit
75 Lower Weldon Street
St. Albans, VT 05479-0001
802-527-3160

AYUDA LEGAL

Si quieres, puedes pagar a un abogado para que te ayude llenar el formulario de solicitud N-400. Si es así, busca en la guía telefónica de tu estado el nombre de *Bar Association* o *Legal Aid Society.* Muchos abogados de inmigración también estás listados en las páginas amarillas de las guías telefónicas. Ten mucho cuidado en elegir abogado. Pregunta a tus amigos o familiares si saben de un abogado que sea bueno.

El *American Immigration Lawyers Association* (AILA) es el lugar que puedes contactar para más información. Tiene una lista de más de 7,200 abogados que practican leyes migratorias. Los miembros del AILA han representado a miles de familias estadounidenses que han solicitado residencia permanente para sus cónyugues, hijos, y otros parientes cercanos para que puedan entrar y residir en los Estados Unidos. Puedes contactar AILA para obtener información sobre un abogado de inmigración a:

American Immigration Lawyers Association (AILA)
918 F Street, NW
Washington, DC 20004
Tel: 202-216-2400
www.aila.org

CAPÍTULO 4

Lecciones de Ciudadanía

Cada una de las veintitrés lecciones en este capítulo te ayudará a pasar el examen de ciudadanía. Trabaja lenta y cuidadosamente a través de todas las lecciones, y haz todos los ejercicios enumerados de cada lección.

Esta es una lista de lo que incluye este capítulo:

LECCIÓN 1

Ramas del Gobierno

PALABRAS CLAVES

ramas: partes separadas

Congreso: gente que hace nuestras leyes

juramento: promesa de decir la verdad

SOBRE LAS RAMAS DEL GOBIERNO

Existen tres **ramas** del gobierno para que de esa manera no sea sólo una persona la que pueda tener demasiado poder. Cada **rama** previene que las otras se vuelvan muy fuertes. Estas tres **ramas** son:

1. Ejecutivo
   - Presidente
   - Vice Presidente
   - Cabinete

2. Legislativo
   - Congreso

3. Judicial
   - La Corte Suprema

La rama Ejecutiva pone en práctica las leyes, **la rama Legislativa** hace las leyes, y **la rama Judicial** explica las leyes.

Turn page for English translation

LESSON 1

Branches of Government

WORDS TO KNOW

branches: separate parts

Congress: people who make our laws

oath: promise to tell the truth

ABOUT THE BRANCHES OF GOVERNMENT

There are three **branches** of government so that no one branch or person can have too much power. Each **branch** keeps the others from getting too strong. The three **branches** are:

1. Executive
   - President
   - Vice President
   - Cabinet

2. Legislative
   - Congress

3. Judicial
   - Supreme Court

The **Executive Branch** carries out the laws, the **Legislative Branch** makes the laws, and the **Judicial Branch** explains the laws.

REPETICIÓN

Dí, repite, en voz alta y muchas veces estas preguntas y respuestas.

1. How many branches are there in the government?
   three (3)

2. What are the three branches of our government?
   executive, legislative, judicial

3. What is the executive branch of our government?
   President, Vice President, Cabinet

4. What is the legislative branch of our government?
   Congress

5. What is the judicial branch of our government?
   Supreme Court

EJERCICIOS

Los siguientes ejercicios han sido diseñados para familiarizarte con el material de esta lección. El verdadero examen de ciudadanía puede ser oral o un examen de respuestas múltiples.

Preguntas de elección múltiple

Marca tus preguntas a estas preguntas en la hoja que sigue. Las respuestas a todos los ejercicios pueden ser encontradas en la última página de esta lección.

1. Ⓐ Ⓑ Ⓒ Ⓓ   4. Ⓐ Ⓑ Ⓒ Ⓓ
2. Ⓐ Ⓑ Ⓒ Ⓓ   5. Ⓐ Ⓑ Ⓒ Ⓓ
3. Ⓐ Ⓑ Ⓒ Ⓓ

1. What is the executive branch?
   A. Congress
   B. Supreme Court
   C. President, Vice President, Cabinet
   D. judicial

2. What is the legislative branch?
   A. Congress
   B. Supreme Court
   C. President, Vice President, Cabinet
   D. judicial

3. What is the judicial branch?
   A. Congress
   B. Supreme Court
   C. President, Vice President, Cabinet
   D. judicial

4. What are the three branches of our government?
   A. Congress, President, Cabinet
   B. executive, judicial, legislative
   C. President, Vice President, Cabinet
   D. executive, President, Congress

5. How many branches are there in the government?
   A. one
   B. two
   C. three
   D. four

Encierra en un círculo la respuesta correcta.

1. What is the judicial branch?
   Congress   Supreme Court

2. How many branches of government are there?
   five   three

3. What is the executive branch?
   Supreme Court   President, Cabinet, Vice President

4. What is the legislative branch?
   Congress   President

5. What are the three branches of government?
   executive, judicial, legislative   federal, state, judicial

Preguntas de Si o No
Encierra **Si** en un círculo si la oración es correcta. Encierra **No** si la oración no es correcta.

Si	No	The President is in the judicial branch of government.
Si	No	The Supreme Court is in the judicial branch of government.
Si	No	There are three branches of government.
Si	No	The Congress is in the executive branch of government.
Si	No	The President is in the executive branch of government.
Si	No	There are five branches of government.

PRACTICA DE DICTADO

Escribe cada oración dos veces. La primera vez, copia la lección. La segunda vez, haz que alguien lea la oración mientras la escribes.

1. I study.

2. I study English.

3. I study citizenship.

1. _____.

1. _____.

2. _____.

2. _____.

3. _____.

3. _____.

PRACTICA PARA LA ENTREVISTA

Esto es lo que puede que oigas en tu entrevista. Lo que sigue es lo que debes hacer y lo que significa.

Entrevistador:	Please stand and raise your right hand.
Lo que tienes que hacer:	Póngase de pie y levante la mano derecha.
¿Qué significa?	Te estás poniendo listo para tomar el juramento.

Entrevistador:	Do you swear that everything you say today will be the truth?
Lo que tienes que hacer:	Responda en voz fuerte, "si."
¿Qué significa?	Has prometido decir la verdad. Has prometido no mentir.
Entrevistador:	Do you promise to tell the truth and nothing but the truth, so help you God?
Lo que tienes que hacer:	Responda en voz fuerte, "si."
¿Qué significa?	Que has prometido decir la verdad y no mentirás.
Entrevistador:	Please sit down.
Lo que tienes que hacer:	Siéntate en tu silla.
¿Qué significa?	El juramento está finalizado.

Di, repite, en voz alta y muchas veces estas preguntas y respuestas.

Pregunta:	Do you understand what an oath is?
Respuesta:	Yes, it is a promise to tell the truth.
Pregunta:	What is your complete name?
Respuesta:	My name is Yolanda Rodriguez Martinez.
Pregunta:	What is your name?
Respuesta:	Yolanda Rodriguez Martinez.

Tu Turno

Haz que alguien te pregunte las preguntas anteriores. Responde con las preguntas que sean para tí correctas.

RESPUESTAS DE LA LECCIÓN 1

Preguntas de elección múltiple
1. C. President, Vice President, Cabinet
2. A. Congress
3. B. Supreme Court
4. B. executive, judicial, legislative
5. C. three

Encierra en un círculo la respuesta correcta.
1. What is the judicial branch?

Congress   (Supreme Court)

2. How many branches of government are there?

five   (three)

3. What is the executive branch?

Supreme Court   (President, Cabinet, Vice President)

4. What is the legislative branch?

(Congress)   President

5. What are the three branches of government?

(executive, judicial, legislative)   federal, state, judicial

Preguntas de Si o No

Si   (No)   The President is in the judicial branch of government.

(Si)   No   The Supreme Court is in the judicial branch of government.

(Si)   No   There are three branches of government.

Si   (No)   Congress is in the executive branch of government.

(Si)   No   The President is in the executive branch of government.

Si   (No)   There are five branches of government.

LECCIÓN 2

La Rama Legislativa

PALABRAS CLAVES

dirección:	donde vives
Capitolio:	donde se reúne el Congreso
trabajo:	empleo o responsabilidad
la rama legislativa:	el Congreso

SOBRE LA RAMA LEGISLATIVA

La **rama Legislativa** del gobierno estadounidense incluye al Congreso. El **trabajo** del Congreso es hacer las leyes. El Congreso incluye el Senado y la Casa de Representantes. El Congreso se reúne en el **Capitolio** en Washington, DC, y es elegido por la gente. El Congreso tiene el poder de declarar Guerra:

- Rama Legislativa
- Congreso (se reúne en el Capitolio y tiene poder de declarar Guerra)
- Senado
- Casa de Representantes

LESSON 2

The Legislative Branch

WORDS TO KNOW

address:	where you live
Capitol:	where Congress meets
job:	work or duty
legislative branch:	Congress

ABOUT THE LEGISLATIVE BRANCH

The **legislative branch** of our government includes Congress. The **job** of Congress is to make laws. Congress includes the Senate and the House of Representatives. Congress meets in the **Capitol** in Washington, DC and is elected by the people. Congress has the power to declare war.

- Legislative Branch
- Congress (meets in Capitol and has power to declare war)
- Senate
- House of Representatives

REPETICIÓN

Di, repite, en voz alta y muchas veces estas preguntas y respuestas.

1. Who makes the laws in the United States?
Congress

2. What is Congress?
Senate and House of Representatives

3. What are the duties of Congress?
to make laws

4. Who elects Congress?
the people

5. Where does Congress meet?
Capitol in Washington, DC

6. Who has the power to declare war?
Congress

7. What is the United States Capitol?
place where Congress meets

EJERCICIOS

Los siguientes ejercicios han sido diseñados para familiarizarte con el material de esta lección. El verdadero examen de ciudadanía puede ser oral o un examen de respuestas múltiples.

Preguntas de elección múltiple

Mark your answers to these test questions on the bubble answer sheet below. The answers to all the exercises are found on the last page of this lesson.

1. (A) (B) (C) (D) **4.** (A) (B) (C) (D)

2. (A) (B) (C) (D) **5.** (A) (B) (C) (D)

3. (A) (B) (C) (D) **6.** (A) (B) (C) (D)

7. (A) (B) (C) (D)

1. What does the legislative branch include?
   A. judicial
   B. Supreme Court
   C. President, Vice President, Cabinet
   D. Congress

2. What does Congress do?
   A. elects the mayor
   B. makes laws
   C. interprets laws
   D. collects taxes

3. What are the two parts of Congress?
   A. Senate and Capitol
   B. Senate and Washington, DC
   C. Senate and House of Representatives
   D. House of Representatives and Capitol

4. Where does Congress meet?
   A. in the White House
   B. in the House in New York City
   C. in the House in Philadelphia, Pennsylvania
   D. in the Capitol in Washington, DC

5. Who elects Congress?
   A. the President
   B. the Vice President
   C. the people
   D. the governor of New York

6. What is the United States Capitol?
   A. the place where Congress meets
   B. the President's official residence
   C. the place where the Supreme Court meets
   D. the office of the executive branch

7. Who has the power to declare war?
   A. President
   B. Congress
   C. Supreme Court
   D. Vice President

Preguntas para agrupar

Responde cada pregunta con la respuesta más apropiada.

____ Who elects Congress?	A. the Capitol in Washington, DC
____ Who makes the laws in the United States?	B. to make laws
	C. the people
____ What is Congress?	D. Senate and House of Representatives
____ What are the duties of Congress?	
____ Where does Congress meet?	E. Congress
____ What does Congress have the power to declare?	F. war

Preguntas de Sio No

Encierra **Si** en un círculo si la oración es correcta. Encierra **No** si la oración no es correcta.

Si   No   Congress makes the laws in the United States.

Si   No   The President has the power to declare war.

Si   No   Congress includes the Senate and the House of Representatives.

Si   No   The duties of Congress are to please the people.

Si   No   The duties of Congress are to make laws.

Si   No   Congress meets in New York City.

Si   No   Congress has the power to declare war.

PRACTICA DE DICTADO

Escribe cada oración dos veces. La primera vez, copia la lección. La segunda vez, haz que alguien lea la oración mientras la escribes.

1. I want to be a citizen.

2. I want to be an American.

1. _____.

1. _____.

2. _____.

2. _____.

Di, repite, en voz alta y muchas veces estas preguntas y respuestas.

Pregunta:	What is your address?
Respuesta:	My address is 423 Tenth Avenue, Brooklyn, New York 11209.
Pregunta:	Where do you live?
Respuesta:	I live at 423 Tenth Avenue, Brooklyn, New York 11209.
Pregunta:	What is your home phone number?
Respuesta:	My home phone number is 718-555-7889.
Pregunta:	What is your telephone number at home?
Respuesta:	It is 718-555-7889.
Pregunta:	Do you have a work telephone number?
Respuesta:	Yes, my work number is 212-555-6000.
Pregunta:	What is your work phone number?
Respuesta:	My work phone number is 212-555-6000.
Pregunta:	Do you have a work number?
Respuesta:	No, I am not currently working.

Tu Turno

Haz que alguien te pregunte las preguntas anteriores. Responde con las preguntas que sean para tí correctas.

RESPUESTAS DE LA LECCIÓN 2

Preguntas de elección múltiple

1. D. Congress
2. B. makes laws
3. C. Senate and House of Representatives
4. D. in the Capitol in Washington, DC
5. C. the people
6. A. the place where Congress meets
7. B. Congress

Preguntas para agrupar

<u>C</u> Who elects Congress?   A. the Capitol in Washington, DC

<u>E</u> Who makes the laws in the   B. to make laws
    United States?   C. the people

<u>D</u> What is Congress?   D. Senate and House of

<u>B</u> What are the duties of Congress?   Representatives

<u>A</u> Where does Congress meet?   E. Congress

<u>F</u> What does Congress have the   F. war
    power to declare?

Preguntas de Si o No

(Si)   No   Congress makes the laws in the United States.

Si   (No)   The President has the power to declare war.

(Si)   No   Congress includes the Senate and the House of Representatives.

Si   (No)   The duties of Congress are to please the people.

(Si)   No   The duties of Congress are to make laws.

Si   (No)   Congress meets in New York City.

(Si)   No   Congress has the power to declare war.

LECCIÓN 3

Senado

PALABRAS CLAVES

ciudadanía: el país en el cual tienes todo derecho a participar de los beneficios y leyes del mismo

re-elegido: puesto en el gobierno mediante elecciones y por segunda vez

senadores: gente que trabaja en el senado.

union: Los Estados Unidos de Norte América

SOBRE EL SENADO

El Congreso está compuesto por el Senado y por la Casa de Representantes. El Senado tiene 100 **senadores**. Hay como 100 **senadores** porque existen 2 **senadores** por cada estado de la **Unión.** Hay 50 estados en la **Unión.** Cada **senador** es elegido por seis años. No existe un límite para el número de veces que un **senador** pueda ser **re-elegido.** Tienes que saber quiénes son los **senadores** del estado en que vives.

Congreso
- Senado
- Casa de Representantes

Senado
- 100 senadores (2 de cada uno de los 50 estados)

Senadores
- Elegidos por 6 años
- No límite para ser re-elegidos
- 2 de cada estado

Turn page for English translation

LESSON 3

Senate

WORDS TO KNOW

citizenship: the country where you have the right to fully participate in the benefits and laws of that country

re-elected: voted into office again

senators: people who work in the Senate

union: United States of America

ABOUT THE SENATE

Congress is made up of the Senate and the House of Representatives. The Senate has 100 **senators**. There are 100 **senators** because there are two **senators** from each state in the **union**. There are fifty states in the **union**. Each **senator** is elected for six years. There is no limit to how many times **senators** can be **re-elected**. You should know who the two **senators** are from your state.

Congress
- Senate
- House of Representatives

Senate
- 100 senators (2 from each of the 50 states)

Senators
- Elected for 6 years
- No limit to re-election
- 2 from each state

REPETICIÓN

Di, repite, en voz alta y muchas veces estas preguntas y respuestas.

1. How many senators are there in Congress?
100 (one hundred)

2. Why are there 100 senators in Congress?
two (2) from each state

3. Who are the two senators from your state?
Pregunta a un profesor, o a un familiar la respuestas a la pregunta.

4. How long do we elect each senator?
six (6) years

5. How many times can a senator be re-elected?
no limit

EJERCICIOS

Los siguientes ejercicios han sido diseñados para familiarizarte con el material de esta lección. El verdadero examen de ciudadanía puede ser oral o un examen de respuestas múltiples.

Preguntas de elección múltiple

Marca tus preguntas a estas preguntas en la hoja que sigue. Las respuestas a todos los ejercicios pueden ser encontradas en la última página de esta lección.

1. (A) (B) (C) (D)   **3.** (A) (B) (C) (D)

2. (A) (B) (C) (D)   **4.** (A) (B) (C) (D)

1. Why are there 100 senators in Congress?
A. there are 100 states in the union
B. there are two senators from each state
C. tradition
D. because that is all that fits in the Senate Gallery

2. How many times can a senator be re-elected?
A. zero
B. one
C. two
D. no limit

3. How many senators are in Congress?
A. 50
B. 100
C. 101
D. 200

4. For how many years is a senator elected?
A. four
B. five
C. six
D. eight

Encierra en un círculo la respuesta correcta.

1. There are _____ senators in Congress.
100   435

2. A senator is elected for _____ years.
six   ten

3. How many times can a senator be re-elected?
no limit   ten

4. There are 100 senators because there are _____ from each state.
two   four

5. The word "union" means _____.
the United States   provinces in Canada

Preguntas de Sio No

Encierra **Si** en un círculo si la oración es correcta. Encierra **No** si la oración no es correcta.

Si   No   A senator is elected for 100 years.

Si   No   There are 100 senators because there are two from each state.

Si   No   There is no limit to how many times a senator can be re-elected.

Si   No   A senator is elected for six years.

Si   No   There are 435 senators in Congress.

PRACTICA DE DICTADO

Escribe cada oración dos veces. La primera vez, copia la lección. La segunda vez, haz que alguien lea la oración mientras la escribes.

1. I live in California.

2. I live with my family.

3. I live in California with my family.

1. _____.

1. _____.

2. _____.

2. _____.

3. _____.

3. _____.

PRACTICA PARA LA ENTREVISTA

Di, repite, en voz alta y muchas veces estas preguntas y respuestas.

Pregunta:	May I see your passport?
Respuesta:	Yes, here it is.
Pregunta:	Do you have your passport with you?
Respuesta:	Yes, I do.
Pregunta:	What is your current citizenship?
Respuesta:	I am currently a citizen of Mexico.
Pregunta:	Your current citizenship is?
Respuesta:	Mexican.

Tu Turno
Haz que alguien te haga las preguntas anteriores. Responde con las preguntas que sean para tí correctas.

RESPUESTAS DE LA LECCIÓN 3

Preguntas de elección múltiple
1. B. there are two senators from each state
2. D. no limit
3. B. 100
4. C. six

Encierra en un círculo la respuesta correcta.
1. There are _____ senators in Congress.
   (100)   435

2. A senator is elected for _____ years.
   (six)   ten

3. How many times can a senator be re-elected?
   (no limit)   ten

4. There are 100 senators because there are _____ from each state.
   (two)   four

5. The word "union" means _____.
   (the United States)   provinces in Canada

Preguntas de Sio No

Si (No)   A senator is elected for 100 years.

(Si) No   There are 100 senators because there are two from each state.

(Si) No   There is no limit to how many times a senator can be re-elected.

(Si) No   A senator is elected for six years.

Si (No)   There are 435 senators in Congress.

LECCIÓN 4

Casa de Representantes

PALABRAS CLAVES

lugar de nacimiento: país donde naciste

representantes: gente que trabaja en la Casa de Representantes

término: el tiempo que alguien trabaja en el gobierno

SOBRE LA CASA DE REPRESENTANTES

El Congreso está compuesto por el Senado y la Casa de Representantes. La Casa de Representantes tiene 435 **miembros**. Si hay mucha gente en un determinado estado, ellos pueden elegir muchos **representantes**. Si hay poca gente en un estado, ellos sólo pueden elegir pocos **representantes**. Cada **representante** es elegido for un **término** de dos años. No hay un límite para el número de veces que un **representante** pueda ser re-elegido.

Casa de Representates
- 435 representantes
- elegidos por el término de 2 años
- no límite en el número de veces que estos puedan ser re-elegidos

Turn page for English translation

LESSON 4

House of Representatives

WORDS TO KNOW

birth place: country where you were born

representatives: people who work in the House of Representatives

term: how long someone works in government

ABOUT THE HOUSE OF REPRESENTATIVES

Congress is made up of the Senate and the House of Representatives. The House of Representatives has 435 **representatives**. If there are many people in a state, they can elect many **representatives**. If there are few people in a state, they can elect only a few **representatives**. Each **representative** is elected for a two-year **term**. There is no limit to how many times **representatives** can be re-elected.

House of Representatives
- 435 representatives
- elected for 2 year terms
- no limit to the number of times they can be re-elected

REPETICIÓN

Di, repite, en voz alta y muchas veces estas preguntas y respuestas.

1. How many representatives are there in Congress?
   435 (four hundred thirty-five)

2. How long do we elect the representatives?
   two (2) years

3. How many times can a representative be re-elected?
   no limit

4. How many representatives does each state have?
   depends on how many people live in the state

EJERCICIOS

Los siguientes ejercicios han sido diseñados para familiarizarte con el material de esta lección. El verdadero examen de ciudadanía puede ser oral o un examen de respuestas múltiples.

Preguntas de elección múltiple

Marca tus preguntas a estas preguntas en la hoja que sigue. Las respuestas a todos los ejercicios pueden ser encontradas en la última página de esta lección.

1. (A) (B) (C) (D)   3. (A) (B) (C) (D)
2. (A) (B) (C) (D)   4. (A) (B) (C) (D)

1. How long do we elect the representatives?
   A. one year
   B. two years
   C. three years
   D. four years

2. How many times can a representative be re-elected?
   A. zero
   B. one
   C. two
   D. no limit

---

3. How many representatives are in Congress?

    A. 100

    B. 101

    C. 435

    D. 450

4. For how many years is a representative elected?

    A. two

    B. four

    C. six

    D. eight

Escribe en los espacios vacios

1. There are _____ representatives in Congress.

    435   100

2. A representative is elected for _____ years.

    six   two

3. There is _____ to the number of times a representative can be re-elected.

    a limit   no limit

4. If there are many people in a state, they can elect _____ representatives.

    many   two

Preguntas de Sio No

Encierra **Si** en un círculo si la oración es correcta. Encierra **No** si la oración no es correcta.

Si	No	A representative is elected for a two-year term.
Si	No	There are 435 representatives because there are two from each state.
Si	No	There is no limit to how many times a representative can be re-elected.
Si	No	A representative is elected for two years.
Si	No	There are 435 representatives in Congress.

PRACTICA DE DICTADO

Escribe cada oración dos veces. La primera vez, copia la lección. La segunda vez, haz que alguien lea la oración mientras la escribes.

1. I want to be an American citizen.

2. I want to be a citizen of the United States.

1. _____.

1. _____.

2. _____.

2. _____.

PRACTICA PARA LA ENTREVISTA

Di, repite, en voz alta y muchas veces estas preguntas y respuestas.

Pregunta:	What is your date of birth?
Respuesta:	I was born on July 12, 1953.
Pregunta:	When were you born?
Respuesta:	On July 12, 1953.
Pregunta:	What is your birth date?
Respuesta:	My birth date is July 12, 1953.
Pregunta:	Where were you born?
Respuesta:	I was born in India.
Pregunta:	What is your place of birth?
Respuesta:	I was born in India.
Pregunta:	What is your birth place?
Respuesta:	I was born in India.

Tu Turno
Haz que alguien te pregunte las preguntas anteriores. Responde con las preguntas que sean para tí correctas.

RESPUESTAS DE LA LECCIÓN 4

Multiple Choice
1. B. two years
2. D. no limit
3. C. 435
4. A. two

Escribe en los espacios vacios
1. There are <u>435</u> representatives in Congress.
2. A representative is elected for <u>two</u> years.
3. There is <u>no limit</u> to the number of times a representative can be re-elected.
4. If there are many people in a state, they can elect <u>many</u> representatives.

Yes or No Question

(Si)   No   A representative is elected for a two-year term.

Si   (No)   There are 435 representatives because there are two from each state.

(Si)   No   There is no limit to how many times a representative can be re-elected.

(Si)   No   A representative is elected for two years.

(Si)   No   There are 435 representatives in Congress.

PRUEBA DE REPASO 1

Marca las respuestas para cada pregunta en la hoja que sigue. Las respuestas de esta prueba se pueden encontrar en la última página de la prueba de repaso.

1. (A) (B) (C) (D)　　9. (A) (B) (C) (D)
2. (A) (B) (C) (D)　　10. (A) (B) (C) (D)
3. (A) (B) (C) (D)　　11. (A) (B) (C) (D)
4. (A) (B) (C) (D)　　12. (A) (B) (C) (D)
5. (A) (B) (C) (D)　　13. (A) (B) (C) (D)
6. (A) (B) (C) (D)　　14. (A) (B) (C) (D)
7. (A) (B) (C) (D)　　15. (A) (B) (C) (D)
8. (A) (B) (C) (D)

1. How many branches of the government are there?
   A. one
   B. two
   C. three
   D. four

2. What is the legislative branch?
   A. Congress
   B. Supreme Court
   C. President
   D. mayor

3. What is the judicial branch?
   A. Congress
   B. President
   C. Vice President
   D. Supreme Court

4. What is the executive branch?
   A. President, Vice President, Cabinet
   B. Congress
   C. Supreme Court
   D. House of Representatives

5. What are the three branches of government?
   A. Supreme Court, President, Congress
   B. executive, legislative, judicial
   C. Senate, House of Representatives, Cabinet
   D. law, federal, Congress

6. Where does Congress meet?
   A. Supreme Court
   B. Capitol in Washington, DC
   C. New York City
   D. White House

7. What is Congress?
   A. President
   B. Senate and House of Representatives
   C. Senate and Supreme Court
   D. governor

8. Who elects Congress?
   A. Electoral College
   B. President
   C. mayor
   D. the people

9. Who makes the laws in the United States?
   A. Supreme Court
   B. President
   C. Congress
   D. mayor

10. What is the job of Congress?
   A. to make laws
   B. to enforce laws
   C. to interpret laws
   D. to collect money

11. Why are there 100 senators in Congress?
    A. two from each state
    B. four from each state
    C. six from each state
    D. seven from each state

12. How many times can a senator be re-elected?
    A. two
    B. four
    C. no limit
    D. five

13. How long do we elect each senator?
    A. three years
    B. two years
    C. six years
    D. four years

14. How many senators are there in Congress?
    A. 100
    B. 435
    C. 600
    D. 50

15. How many representatives are there in Congress?
    A. 100
    B. 435
    C. 600
    D. 50

RESPUESTAS DE LA LECCIÓN PRUEBA DE REPASO 1

1. C. three
2. A. Congress
3. D. Supreme Court
4. A. President, Vice President, Cabinet
5. B. executive, legislative, judicial
6. B. Capitol in Washington, DC
7. B. Senate and House of Representatives
8. D. the people
9. C. Congress
10. A. to make laws
11. A. two from each state
12. C. no limit
13. C. six years
14. A. 100
15. B. 435

LECCIÓN 5

La Rama Judicial

PALABRAS CLAVES

nombrado: elegido o seleccionado

jefe de justicia: el que encabeza la Corte Suprema

interpretar: explicar

la rama judicial: la parte del gobierno que incluye la Corte Suprema

estado civil: si estás soltero, casado, o divorciado

Corte Suprema: la corte más alta en los Estados Unidos

SOBRE LA RAMA JUDICIAL

La **rama judicial** está compuesta por la **Corte Suprema.** La función de la **Corte Suprema** es **interpretar** las leyes. La **Corte Suprema** tiene nueve jueces y el **jefe de justicia** es William Rehnquist. Los nueve jueces son **nombrados** por el presidente. La **Corte Suprema** es la corte más alta de los Estados Unidos. Los jueces de la **Corte Suprema** pueden ejercer este cargo hasta que mueran. Los jueces de la **Corte Suprema** trabajan en el edificio de la **Corte Suprema.**

Rama Judicial

Corte Suprema
- Corte más alta de los Estados Unidos
- Interpreta la leyes
- Trabaja en el edificio de la Corte Suprema
- Tiene 9 jueces
- El juez principal es William Rehnquist
- Los jueces ejercen esta función hasta que mueran

Turn page for English translation

LESSON 5

The Judicial Branch

WORDS TO KNOW

appointed: chosen or selected

chief justice: head of the Supreme Court

interpret: to explain

judicial branch: the part of the government that includes the Supreme Court

marital status: if you are single, married, or divorced

Supreme Court: highest court in the United States

ABOUT THE JUDICIAL BRANCH

The **judicial branch** is made up of the **Supreme Court**. The job of the **Supreme Court** is to **interpret** the laws. The **Supreme Court** has nine justices and the **chief justice** is William Rehnquist. The nine justices are **appointed** by the President. The **Supreme Court** is the highest court in the United States. The **Supreme Court** justices can work in this job until they die. The **Supreme Court** justices work in the **Supreme Court** building.

Judicial Branch

Supreme Court
- Highest court in the U.S.
- Interprets laws
- Works in Supreme Court Building
- Has 9 justices
- Chief Justice is William Rehnquist
- Justices hold this position until they die

REPETICIÓN

Di, repite, en voz alta y muchas veces estas preguntas y respuestas.

1. What are the duties of the Supreme Court?
   to interpret laws

2. Who is the chief justice of the Supreme Court?
   William Rehnquist

3. Who selects the Supreme Court justices?
   President

4. How many Supreme Court justices are there?
   nine (9)

5. What is the highest court in the United States?
   Supreme Court

EJERCICIOS

Los siguientes ejercicios han sido diseñados para familiarizarte con el material de esta lección. El verdadero examen de ciudadanía puede ser oral o un examen de respuestas múltiples.

Preguntas de elección múltiple

Marca tus preguntas a estas preguntas en la hoja que sigue. Las respuestas a todos los ejercicios pueden ser encontradas en la última página de esta lección.

1. (A) (B) (C) (D)   4. (A) (B) (C) (D)
2. (A) (B) (C) (D)   5. (A) (B) (C) (D)
3. (A) (B) (C) (D)

1. How many Supreme Court justices are there?
   A. eight
   B. nine
   C. ten
   D. eleven

2. Who appoints the Supreme Court justices?
  A. the people
  B. Congress
  C. the President
  D. the Vice President

3. What is the job of the Supreme Court justices?
  A. to make laws
  B. to collect money
  C. to interpret laws
  D. to entertain the public

4. Who is the chief justice of the Supreme Court?
  A. Bill Clinton
  B. Al Gore
  C. Judge Judy
  D. William Rehnquist

5. What is the highest court in the United States?
  A. Supreme Court
  B. Judges Court
  C. White House
  D. Capitol

Escribe en los espacios vacíos

1. The _____ selects the Supreme Court justices.
  President   Cabinet

2. The duty of the Supreme Court is to _____ laws.
  interpret   make

3. The _____ Court is the highest court in the United States.
  State   Supreme

4. There are _____ justices on the Supreme Court.
  ten   nine

5. William _____ is the chief justice of the Supreme Court.
  Clinton   Rehnquist

Preguntas de Si o No

Encierra **Si** en un círculo si la oración es correcta. Encierra **No** si la oración no es correcta.

Si   No   The duty of the Supreme Court is to make laws.

Si   No   The duty of the Supreme Court is to interpret laws.

Si   No   There are nine justices on the Supreme Court.

Si   No   William Rehnquist is the Vice President.

Si   No   The President appoints the Supreme Court justices.

PRACTICA DE DICTADO

Escribe cada oración dos veces. La primera vez, copia la lección. La segunda vez, haz que alguien lea la oración mientras la escribes.

1. I drive to work.

2. I drive my car to work.

3. I like to drive my car to work.

1. _____.

1. _____.

2. _____.

2. _____.

3. _____.

3. _____.

PRACTICA PARA LA ENTREVISTA

Di, repite, en voz alta y muchas veces estas preguntas y respuestas.

Pregunta:	What is your marital status?
Respuesta:	I am married.

Pregunta:	What is your marital status?
Respuesta:	I am divorced.

Pregunta:	Are you married?
Respuesta:	No, I am single.
Pregunta:	Have you ever been married previously?
Respuesta:	Yes, I was married for one year when I lived in Mexico.
Pregunta:	Is your husband a United States citizen?
Respuesta:	No, he is not a United States citizen.
Pregunta:	Is your wife a United States citizen?
Respuesta:	Yes, she is.
Pregunta:	Why did you get a divorce?
Respuesta:	We fought too much.
Pregunta:	How long have you been married?
Respuesta:	I have been married for ten years.

Tu Turno

Haz que alguien te haga las preguntas anteriores. Responde con las preguntas que sean para tí correctas.

RESPUESTAS DE LA LECCIÓN 5

Preguntas de elección múltiple
1. B. nine
2. C. the President
3. C. to interpret laws
4. D. William Rehnquist
5. A. Supreme Court

Escribe en los espacios vacíos
1. The <u>President</u> selects the Supreme Court justices.
2. The duty of the Supreme Court is to <u>interpret</u> laws.
3. The <u>Supreme</u> Court is the highest court in the United States.
4. There are <u>nine</u> justices on the Supreme Court.
5. William <u>Rehnquist</u> is the chief justice of the Supreme Court.

Preguntas de Si o No

Si (No)   The duty of the Supreme Court is to make laws.

(Si) No   The duty of the Supreme Court is to interpret laws.

(Si) No   There are nine justices on the Supreme Court.

Si (No)   William Rehnquist is the Vice President.

(Si) No   The President appoints the Supreme Court justices.

LECCIÓN 6

La Rama Ejecutiva

PALABRAS CLAVES

Colegio Electoral: grupo que elije al presidente

la rama judicial: parte del gobierno compuesta por el Presidente, Vice Presidente, y el Cabinete.

puerto de entrada: lugar al que llegó a su entrada a los Estados Unidos

SOBRE LA RAMA JUDICIAL

El trabajo de la **rama judicial** es hacer cumplir la ley. Incluye el Presidente, Vice Presidente, y el Cabinete. El primer presidente de los Estados Unidos fué George Washington. El presidente actual es George W. Bush, y el vice presidente es Richard Cheney. El presidente es elegido por un periodo de cuatro años por el **colegio electoral.**

Rama Ejecutiva
- Presidente
- Vice Presidente
- Cabinete

Presidente
- Elegido por un término de 4 años
- Elegido por el Colegio Electoral

LESSON 6

The Executive Branch

WORDS TO KNOW

Electoral College: group who elects the President

executive branch: part of government made up of the President, Vice President, and Cabinet

port of entry: place where you arrived in the country

ABOUT THE EXECUTIVE BRANCH

The job of the **executive branch** is to enforce the law. It includes the President, Vice President, and Cabinet. The first President of the United States was George Washington. The President today is George W. Bush, and the Vice President is Richard Cheney. The President is elected for a four-year term and is elected by the **Electoral College**.

Executive Branch
- President
- Vice President
- Cabinet

President
- Elected for 4 year term
- Elected by Electoral College

REPETICIÓN

Di, repite, en voz alta y muchas veces estas preguntas y respuestas.

1. What is the job of the executive branch?
to enforce the law

2. Who was the first President of the United States?
George Washington

3. Who is the President of the United States today?
George W. Bush

4. Who is the Vice President today?
Richard Cheney

5. Who elects the President of the United States?
the Electoral College

6. How long do we elect the President?
four (4) years

EJERCICIOS

Los siguientes ejercicios han sido diseñados para familiarizarte con el material de esta lección. El verdadero examen de ciudadanía puede ser oral o un examen de respuestas múltiples.

Preguntas de elección múltiple
Marca tus preguntas a estas preguntas en la hoja que sigue. Las respuestas a todos los ejercicios pueden ser encontradas en la última página de esta lección.

1. Ⓐ Ⓑ Ⓒ Ⓓ   **4.** Ⓐ Ⓑ Ⓒ Ⓓ

2. Ⓐ Ⓑ Ⓒ Ⓓ   **5.** Ⓐ Ⓑ Ⓒ Ⓓ

3. Ⓐ Ⓑ Ⓒ Ⓓ

1. Who elects the President of the United States?
A. Senate
B. Congress
C. Electoral College
D. Cabinet

2. Who was the first President of the United States?
   A. Bill Clinton
   B. William Rehnquist
   C. Abraham Lincoln
   D. George Washington

3. What is the duty of the executive branch?
   A. to enforce laws
   B. to interpret laws
   C. to collect money
   D. to buy land

4. How long do we elect the President?
   A. one year
   B. two years
   C. three years
   D. four years

5. Who is the Vice President today?
   A. Richard Cheney
   B. Al Gore
   C. William Rehnquist
   D. George Washington

Preguntas para agrupar

Responde cada pregunta con la respuesta más apropiada.

_____ first President of the United States   A. four years
_____ Vice President   B. George W. Bush
_____ how long the President is elected   C. Electoral College
_____ President today   D. Richard Cheney
_____ elects the President   E. George Washington
_____ duty of executive branch   F. enforce the law

Preguntas de Sí o No

Encierra **Sí** en un círculo si la oración es correcta. Encierra **No** si la oración no es correcta.

Sí   No   The duty of the executive branch is to enforce laws.

Sí   No   The duty of the executive branch is to interpret laws.

Sí   No   George Washington was the first President of the United States.

Sí   No   Bill Clinton is the Vice President today.

Si No   The President is elected by the Electoral College.

Si No   The President is elected for four years.

PRACTICA DE DICTADO

Escribe cada oración dos veces. La primera vez, copia la lección. La segunda vez, haz que alguien lea la oración mientras la escribes.

1. I take the bus.

2. I take the bus to work.

3. I like to take the bus.

1. _____.

1. _____.

2. _____.

2. _____.

3. _____.

3. _____.

PRACTICA PARA LA ENTREVISTA

Dí, repite, en voz alta y muchas veces estas preguntas y respuestas.

Pregunta: How long have you been a Permanent Resident of the United States?

Respuesta: I have been a resident for ten years.

Pregunta: When did you first come to the United States?

Respuesta: I arrived in the United States in 1989.

Pregunta: On what date did you enter the United States?

Respuesta: I arrived in the United States on September 5, 1989.

Pregunta: How long have you lived in the United States?

Respuesta: I have lived in the United States for ten years.

Pregunta:	Where did you enter the United States?
Respuesta:	I entered the United States in New York City.
Pregunta:	What was your port of entry?
Respuesta:	JFK airport in New York City.
Pregunta:	In what port of entry did you arrive in America?
Respuesta:	My port of entry was the Los Angeles airport.
Pregunta:	What was your port of entry?
Respuesta:	I crossed the United States border near Seattle, Washington.
Pregunta:	When did you become a Permanent Resident?
Respuesta:	I became a Permanent Resident in 1990.
Pregunta:	In what year did you arrive in the United States?
Respuesta:	I came to the United States in 1989.

Tu Turno

Haz que alguien te haga las preguntas anteriores. Responde con las preguntas que
sean para tí correctas.

RESPUESTAS DE LA LECCIÓN 6

Preguntas de elección múltiple
1. C. Electoral College
2. D. George Washington
3. A. to enforce laws
4. D. four years
5. A. Richard Cheney

Preguntas para agrupar

_E_ first President of the United States   A. four years
_D_ Vice President   B. George W. Bush
_A_ how long the President is elected   C. Electoral College
_B_ President today   D. Richard Cheney
_C_ elects the President   E. George Washington
_F_ duty of executive branch   F. enforce the law

Preguntas de Si o No

(Si)   No   The duty of the executive branch is to enforce laws.

Si   (No)   The duty of the executive branch is to interpret laws.

(Si)   No   George Washington was the first President of the United States.

Si   (No)   Bill Clinton is the Vice President today.

(Si)   No   The President is elected by the Electoral College.

(Si)   No   The President is elected for four years.

LECCIÓN 7

Oficina del Presidente

PALABRAS CLAVES

consejo: dar ayuda a alguien

Gabinete: catorce personas que ayudan al presidente a hacer decisiones

empleador: el nombre de la persona o la compañía para la que trabajas

ciudadano de nacimiento: una persona que nace en un país

ocupación: el nombre del trabajo que hace

SOBRE LA OFICINA DEL PRESIDENTE

La rama ejecutiva del gobierno incluye el Presidente, Vice Presidente, y el Cabinete. Para llegar a ser presidente, uno tiene que:

- ser un **ciudadano nacido** en los Estados Unidos
- tener por lo menos 35 años de edad
- haber vivido en los Estados Unidos por lo menos catorce años

El **Gabinete** es un grupo especial de personas que **aconsejan** al presidente. El presidente puede servir por dos términos. Si el presidente muere, el Vice Presidente llega a ser presidente. Si ambos, el presidente y el vice presidente fallecen, entonces el Porta Voz de la Casa de Representantes llega a ocupar el cargo de Presidente.

Turn page for English translation

LESSON 7

Office of the President

WORDS TO KNOW

advises: gives help to

Cabinet: fourteen people who help the President make decisions

employer: the name of the company or person you work for

natural born citizen: person who is born in a country

occupation: the name of your job

ABOUT THE OFFICE OF THE PRESIDENT

The executive branch of the government includes the President, Vice President, and Cabinet. To become President, you need to:

- be a **natural born citizen** of the U.S.
- be at least thirty-five years old
- have lived in the U.S. for fourteen years

The **Cabinet** is a special group of people that **advises** the President. The President can serve two terms. If the President dies, the Vice President becomes President. If both the President and the Vice President die, then the Speaker of the House of Representatives becomes President.

REPETICIÓN

Di, repite, en voz alta y muchas veces estas preguntas y respuestas.

1. Who becomes President of the United States if the President dies?
Vice President

2. How many terms can a President serve?
two (2)

3. Who becomes President of the United States if the President and Vice President die?
Speaker of the House of Representatives

4. What are the requirements to be President?
natural born citizen of the United States, thirty-five (35) years old, lived in the U.S. fourteen (14) years

5. What special group advises the President?
Cabinet

EJERCICIOS

Los siguientes ejercicios han sido diseñados para familiarizarte con el material de esta lección. El verdadero examen de ciudadanía puede ser oral o un examen de respuestas múltiples.

Preguntas de elección múltiple
Marca tus preguntas a estas preguntas en la hoja que sigue. Las respuestas a todos los ejercicios pueden ser encontradas en la última página de esta lección.

1. (A) (B) (C) (D) **4.** (A) (B) (C) (D)

2. (A) (B) (C) (D) **5.** (A) (B) (C) (D)

3. (A) (B) (C) (D)

1. A President can serve how many terms?
A. one
B. two
C. three
D. four

---

2. Who becomes the President if the President dies?
   A. Vice President
   B. First Lady
   C. a Cabinet member
   D. the Supreme Court Justice

3. What special group advises the President?
   A. Congress
   B. Supreme Court
   C. taxpayers
   D. Cabinet

4. Who becomes President if both the President and the Vice President die?
   A. spouse of the President
   B. chief justice of the Supreme Court
   C. the Senate Majority Leader
   D. Speaker of the House of Representatives

5. What is one requirement to be President?
   A. born in Europe
   B. thirty-five years old
   C. lived in the United States for five years
   D. speak Latin

Encierra en un círculo la respuesta correcta.

1. What is one requirement to be President?
   born in Canada   natural born citizen of the U.S.

2. Who becomes President if the President dies?
   First Lady   Vice President

3. What special group advises the President?
   Congress   Cabinet

4. Who becomes President if the President and Vice President die?
   Speaker of the House of Representatives   Congress

5. How many terms can a President serve?
    two   three

Preguntas de Si o No

Encierra **Si** en un círculo si la oración es correcta. Encierra **No** si la oración no es correcta.

Si	No	To become President, you must be a natural born citizen of the U.S.
Si	No	The Cabinet advises the President.
Si	No	The duty of the executive branch is to enforce laws.
Si	No	The First Lady becomes President if the President dies.
Si	No	The executive branch of the government includes the President, Vice President, and Cabinet.
Si	No	The President can serve two terms in office.
Si	No	To become President, you must be at least fifty years old.

PRACTICA DE DICTADO

Escribe cada oración dos veces. La primera vez, copia la lección. La segunda vez, haz que alguien lea la oración mientras la escribes.

1. I go to school.

2. My children go to school.

3. My children and I go to school.

1. _____.

1. _____.

2. _____.

2. _____.

3. _____.

3. _____.

PRACTICA PARA LA ENTREVISTA

Di, repite, en voz alta y muchas veces estas preguntas y respuestas.

Pregunta: Who is your employer?
Respuesta: I am unemployed right now.

Pregunta: Why aren't you working?
Respuesta: I was laid off from my last job, and I'm looking for a new job.

Pregunta: Who is your current employer?
Respuesta: My employer is Machines, Inc.

Pregunta: Whom do you currently work for?
Respuesta: I work for Machines, Inc.

Pregunta: Are you currently working?
Respuesta: Yes, I work for Machines, Inc.

Pregunta: What kind of work do you do?
Respuesta: I work for Machines, Inc. as a factory worker.

Pregunta: Do you have a job?
Respuesta: Yes, I work at Machines, Inc.

Pregunta: What is your occupation?
Respuesta: I am a factory worker.

Pregunta: What kind of income do you have?
Respuesta: I get an income from working for Machines, Inc.

Pregunta: How do you support yourself?
Respuesta: I work for Machines, Inc.

Pregunta: How long have you held this job?
Respuesta: I have had this job for three years.

Pregunta: Who was your employer before that?
Respuesta: I used to work for Southwest Airlines.

Pregunta: What job did you have there?
Respuesta: I worked as a shipping clerk.

Tu Turno

Haz que alguien te haga las preguntas anteriores. Responde con las preguntas que sean para tí correctas.

RESPUESTAS DE LA LECCIÓN 7

Preguntas de elección múltiple
1. B. two
2. A. Vice President
3. D. Cabinet
4. D. Speaker of the House of Representatives
5. B. thirty-five years old

Encierra en un círculo la respuesta correcta.
1. What is one requirement to be President?
   born in Canada   (natural born citizen of the U.S.)

2. Who becomes President if the President dies?
   First Lady   (Vice President)

3. What special group advises the President?
   Congress   (Cabinet)

4. Who becomes President if the President and Vice President die?
   (Speaker of the House of Representatives)   Congress

5. How many terms can a President serve?
   (two)   three

Preguntas de Si o No

(Si) No   To become President, you must be a natural born citizen of the U.S.

(Si) No   The Cabinet advises the President.

(Si) No   The duty of the executive branch is to enforce laws.

Si (No)   The First Lady becomes President if the President dies.

(Si) No   The executive branch of the government includes the President, Vice President, and Cabinet.

(Si) No   The President can serve two terms in office.

Si (No)   To become President, you must be at least fifty years old.

PRUEBA DE REPASO 2

Marca las respuestas para cada pregunta en la hoja que sigue. Las repuestas de esta prueba se pueden encontrar en la última página de la prueba de repaso.

1. Ⓐ Ⓑ Ⓒ Ⓓ   8. Ⓐ Ⓑ Ⓒ Ⓓ
2. Ⓐ Ⓑ Ⓒ Ⓓ   9. Ⓐ Ⓑ Ⓒ Ⓓ
3. Ⓐ Ⓑ Ⓒ Ⓓ   10. Ⓐ Ⓑ Ⓒ Ⓓ
4. Ⓐ Ⓑ Ⓒ Ⓓ   11. Ⓐ Ⓑ Ⓒ Ⓓ
5. Ⓐ Ⓑ Ⓒ Ⓓ   12. Ⓐ Ⓑ Ⓒ Ⓓ
6. Ⓐ Ⓑ Ⓒ Ⓓ   13. Ⓐ Ⓑ Ⓒ Ⓓ
7. Ⓐ Ⓑ Ⓒ Ⓓ   14. Ⓐ Ⓑ Ⓒ Ⓓ

1. How many times can a representative be re-elected?
A. one
B. two
C. three
D. no limit

2. How long do we elect the representatives?
A. two years
B. three years
C. four years
D. five years

3. How many representatives are there in Congress?
A. 435
B. 100
C. 2
D. 500

4. What are the duties of the Supreme Court?
A. enforce the laws
B. make laws
C. interpret laws
D. declare war

5. Who is the chief justice of the Supreme Court?
A. William Rehnquist
B. Bill Clinton
C. Al Gore
D. Janet Reno

6. Who selects the Supreme Court justices?
A. President
B. Congress
C. Vice President
D. Supreme Court

7. How many Supreme Court justices are there?
A. one
B. five
C. seven
D. nine

8. What is the highest court in the United States?
A. Supreme Court
B. Federal Court
C. City Court
D. State Court

9. How long do we elect the President?
A. two years
B. six years
C. four years
D. three years

10. Who elects the President?
A. Congress
B. Electoral College
C. Supreme Court
D. mayor

11. Who is the Vice President today?
A. Al Gore
B. Richard Cheney
C. Bill Clinton
D. Henry Kissinger

12. Who is the President of the United States today?
   A. George W. Bush
   B. Bill Clinton
   C. William Rehnquist
   D. Al Gore

13. Who was the first President of the United States?
   A. Thomas Jefferson
   B. Bill Clinton
   C. George Washington
   D. Abraham Lincoln

14. What is the job of the executive branch?
   A. make laws
   B. interpret laws
   C. enforce laws
   D. vote

RESPUESTAS DE LA LECCIÓN PRUEBA DE REPASO 2

1. D. no limit
2. A. two years
3. A. 435
4. C. interpret laws
5. A. William Rehnquist
6. A. President
7. D. nine
8. A. Supreme Court
9. C. four years
10. B. Electoral College
11. B. Richard Cheney
12. A. George W. Bush
13. C. George Washington
14. C. enforce laws

LECCIÓN 8

Más acerca del Presidente

PALABRAS CLAVES

nacido: cuando un bebé llega a este mundo

inaugurado: puesto en oficina a través de un juramento

Casa Blanca: lugar donde vive el presidente mientras dura su mandato

SOBRE EL PRESIDENTE

El presidente es la cabeza ejecutiva de los Estados Unidos. Nosotros votamos por el presidente en Noviembre. Luego, en Enero, el Nuevo presidente asume su mandato. Durante el término como presidente, éste vive en la **Casa Blanca** en Washington, DC.

Presidente
- Elegido en Noviembre
- Inaugurado en Enero
- Vive en la Casa Blanca, en Washington, DC

LESSON 8

More about the President

WORDS TO KNOW

born: when a baby comes into the world

inaugurated: sworn into office

White House: place where the President lives while serving as President

ABOUT THE PRESIDENT

The President is the head executive of the United States. We vote for the President in November. Then, in January, the new President is **inaugurated**. During the President's term of office, the President lives in the **White House** in Washington, DC.

President
- Elected in November
- Inaugurated in January
- Lives in White House in Washington, DC

REPETICIÓN

Di, repite, en voz alta y muchas veces estas preguntas y respuestas.

1. What is the White House?
President's official home

2. Where is the White House located?
Washington, DC

3. In what month do we vote for the President?
November

4. In what month is the new President inaugurated?
January

5. What is the name of the President's official home?
White House

EJERCICIOS

Los siguientes ejercicios han sido diseñados para familiarizarte con el material de esta lección. El verdadero examen de ciudadanía puede ser oral o un examen de respuestas múltiples.

Preguntas de elección múltiple

Marca tus preguntas a estas preguntas en la hoja que sigue. Las respuestas a todos los ejercicios pueden ser encontradas en la última página de esta lección.

1. (A) (B) (C) (D)   **4.** (A) (B) (C) (D)

2. (A) (B) (C) (D)   **5.** (A) (B) (C) (D)

3. (A) (B) (C) (D)

1. We vote for the President in which month?
A. October
B. November
C. December
D. January

2. The President is inaugurated in which month?
   A. October
   B. November
   C. December
   D. January

3. What is the President's official home called?
   A. Capitol
   B. White House
   C. Supreme Court
   D. Oval Office

4. Where is the White House located?
   A. Washington, DC
   B. New York, NY
   C. Los Angeles, CA
   D. Philadelphia, PA

5. What happens in November?
   A. the President is inaugurated
   B. our taxes are due
   C. we vote for the President
   D. the President moves into the White House

Preguntas para agrupar
Responde cada pregunta con la respuesta más apropiada.

_____ the President's official home   A. January

_____ we vote for the President during this month   B. White House

_____ the President is inaugurated during this month   C. Washington, DC

_____ the White House is located here   D. November

Preguntas de Si o No
Encierra **Si** en un círculo si la oración es correcta. Encierra **No** si la oración no es correcta.

Si   No   The White House is located in Philadelphia, PA.

Si   No   The White House is the President's official home.

Si   No   The President is inaugurated in November.

Si   No   We vote for the President in January.

Si	No	The Cabinet is the President's official home.
Si	No	The White House is located in Washington, DC.
Si	No	The President is inaugurated in January.
Si	No	We vote for the President in November.

PRACTICA DE DICTADO

Escribe cada oración dos veces. La primera vez, copia la lección. La segunda vez, haz que alguien lea la oración mientras la escribes.

1. The little girl is happy.

2. My family is happy to be in America.

3. The little girl and my family are happy.

1. _____.

1. _____.

2. _____.

2. _____.

3. _____.

3. _____.

PRACTICA PARA LA ENTREVISTA

Dí, repite, en voz alta y muchas veces estas preguntas y respuestas.

Pregunta:	How many children do you have?
Respuesta:	I have three children.

Pregunta:	Do your children live with you?
Respuesta:	Yes, my children live in my home.

Pregunta:	How many people live in your house?
Respuesta:	Five people: myself, my husband, and three children.

Pregunta:	Who do you live with?
Respuesta:	I live with my husband and three children.
Pregunta:	Where do your children live?
Respuesta:	My children live with me in Brooklyn, New York.
Pregunta:	Did any of your children stay in your native country?
Respuesta:	No, all of my children live with me here in Brooklyn.
Pregunta:	When were your children born?
Respuesta:	One was born in 1992, one in 1994, and one in 1997.
Pregunta:	Were they all born in the United States?
Respuesta:	Yes, they were born in America.

Tu Turno

Haz que alguien te haga las preguntas anteriores. Responde con las preguntas que sean para tí correctas.

RESPUESTAS DE LA LECCIÓN 8

Preguntas de elección múltiple

1. B. November
2. D. January
3. B. White House
4. A. Washington, DC
5. C. we vote for the President

Preguntas para agrupar

<u>B</u> the President's official home

<u>D</u> we vote for the President during this month

<u>A</u> the President is inaugurated during this month

<u>C</u> the White House is located here

A. January
B. White House
C. Washington, DC
D. November

Preguntas de Si o No

Si (No) The White House is located in Philadelphia, PA.

(Si) No The White House is the President's official home.

Si (No) The President is inaugurated in November.

Si (No) We vote for the President in January.

Si (No) The Cabinet is the President's official home.

(Si) No The White House is located in Washington, DC.

(Si) No The President is inaugurated in January.

(Si) No We vote for the President in November.

LECCIÓN 9

Autoridades Ejecutivas

PALABRAS CLAVES

deportado: en la corte, un juez ordena que regreses a tu país de origen

gobernador: líder de un estado

autoridad del ejecutivo: el líder o la persona a cargo

alcalde: líder de una ciudad

SOBRE LAS AUTORIDADES EJECUTIVAS

Las **autoridad ejecutiva** de los Estados Unidos es el Presidente. El presidente firma las declaraciones y las convierte en ley. El presidente es también comandante y jefe de las fuerzas armadas de los Estados Unidos. George Washington fue el primer comandante y jefe de las fuerzas armadas estadounidenses. La autoridad ejecutiva de un estado es el **gobernador.** La autoridad ejecutiva de una ciudad es el **alcalde.**

Autoridad Ejecutiva de los Estados Unidos
- Presidente
  - Firma declaraciones y las hace ley
  - Comandante y jefe de las fuerzas armadas de los Estados Unidos

Autoridad Ejecutiva de un Estado
- Gobernador

Autoridad Ejecutiva de una Ciudad
- Alcalde

Turn page for English translation

LESSON 9

 *Head Executives*

WORDS TO KNOW

deported: a judge in court ordered you to go back to your first country

governor: leader of a state

head executive: the leader or person in charge

mayor: leader of a city

ABOUT HEAD EXECUTIVES

The **head executive** of the United States is the President. The President signs bills into law. The President is also commander in chief of the U.S. military. George Washington was the first commander in chief of the U.S. military. The head executive of a state is the **governor**. The head executive of a city is a **mayor**.

Head Executive of the United States
- President
  - Signs bills into law
  - Commander in chief of the U.S. military

Head Executive of a State
- Governor

Head Executive of City
- Mayor

REPETICIÓN

Di, repite, en voz alta y muchas veces estas preguntas y respuestas.

1. What is the head executive of a state government called?
   governor

2. What is the head executive of a city government called?
   mayor

3. Who signs bills into law?
   President

4. Who is commander in chief of the U.S. military?
   President

5. Who was the first commander in chief of the U.S. military?
   George Washington

EJERCICIOS

Los siguientes ejercicios han sido diseñados para familiarizarte con el material de esta lección. El verdadero examen de ciudadanía puede ser oral o un examen de respuestas múltiples.

Preguntas de elección múltiple

Marca tus preguntas a estas preguntas en la hoja que sigue. Las respuestas a todos los ejercicios pueden ser encontradas en la última página de esta lección.

1. Ⓐ Ⓑ Ⓒ Ⓓ   4. Ⓐ Ⓑ Ⓒ Ⓓ
2. Ⓐ Ⓑ Ⓒ Ⓓ   5. Ⓐ Ⓑ Ⓒ Ⓓ
3. Ⓐ Ⓑ Ⓒ Ⓓ   6. Ⓐ Ⓑ Ⓒ Ⓓ
7. Ⓐ Ⓑ Ⓒ Ⓓ

1. Who signs bills into law?
   A. President
   B. Vice President
   C. Speaker of the House
   D. Congress

2. Who was the first commander in chief of the U.S. military?
A. Bill Clinton
B. William Rehnquist
C. Abraham Lincoln
D. George Washington

3. What is the head of a city government called?
A. President
B. governor
C. mayor
D. Cabinet

4. What is the head of a state government called?
A. President
B. governor
C. mayor
D. Cabinet

5. Who is commander in chief of the U.S. military?
A. Al Gore
B. George W. Bush
C. William Rehnquist
D. George Washington

Escribe en los espacios vacios

1. The _____ signs a bill into law.
Congress   President

2. The head executive of a city government is the _____.
governor   mayor

3. The _____ is commander in chief of the U.S. military.
President   citizen

4. The _____ is head executive of a state government.
President   governor

5. The first commander in chief of the U.S. military was _____.
George Washington   Al Gore

Preguntas de Si o No

Encierra **Si** en un círculo si la oración es correcta. Encierra **No** si la oración no es correcta.

Si	No	The governor is the head executive of a city government.
Si	No	The President signs a bill into law.
Si	No	George Washington was the first commander in chief of the U.S. military.
Si	No	The mayor is the head executive of a city government.
Si	No	George W. Bush is the commander in chief of the U.S. military today.
Si	No	The President is the head executive of the United States.
Si	No	The mayor is the head executive of a state government.

PRACTICA DE DICTADO

Escribe cada oración dos veces. La primera vez, copia la lección. La segunda vez, haz que alguien lea la oración mientras la escribes.

1. I believe in freedom.
2. I believe in the Constitution.
3. I believe in freedom and the Constitution.

1. _____.
1. _____.
2. _____.
2. _____.
3. _____.
3. _____.

PRACTICA PARA LA ENTREVISTA

Di, repite, en voz alta y muchas veces estas preguntas y respuestas.

Pregunta:	How many times have you left the United States since you became a Permanent Resident?
Respuesta:	I went out of the United States only one time.
Pregunta:	How long were you away?
Respuesta:	I was gone for three weeks.
Pregunta:	Where did you go?
Respuesta:	I went to visit my aunt in Poland.
Pregunta:	Why did you leave the United States?
Respuesta:	I wanted to visit my aunt in Poland because she was dying.
Pregunta:	Since becoming a Permanent Resident, have you ever left the United States?
Respuesta:	I left only once to go visit my grandmother in Mexico.
Pregunta:	When was the last time you left the United States?
Respuesta:	I went to Canada two years ago.
Pregunta:	Have you left the United States since you became a Permanent Resident?
Respuesta:	No, I've never left the United States.
Pregunta:	Since coming to the U.S., have you traveled to any other country?
Respuesta:	No, I've never left the United States.
Pregunta:	Have you visited any other country since becoming a Permanent Resident?
Respuesta:	Yes, I went to Poland to visit my aunt one time.
Pregunta:	Have you ever been deported by the Immigration office?
Respuesta:	No, I have never been ordered to leave America.
Pregunta:	Were you ever ordered to leave the United States?
Respuesta:	No, I have never been deported.

Tu Turno
Haz que alguien te haga las preguntas anteriores. Responde con las preguntas que sean para tí correctas.

RESPUESTAS DE LA LECCIÓN 9

Preguntas de elección múltiple
1. A. President
2. D. George Washington
3. C. mayor
4. B. governor
5. B. George W. Bush

Escribe en los espacios vacíos
1. The <u>President</u> signs a bill into law.
2. The head executive of a city government is the <u>mayor</u>.
3. The <u>President</u> is commander in chief of the U.S. military.
4. The <u>governor</u> is head executive of a state government.
5. The first commander in chief of the U.S. military was <u>George Washington</u>.

Yes or No Answers

Si **(No)** The governor is the head executive of a city government.

(Si) No The President signs a bill into law.

(Si) No George Washington was the first commander in chief of the U.S. military.

(Si) No The mayor is the head executive of a city government.

Si **(No)** Bill Clinton is the commander in chief of the U.S. military today.

(Si) No The President is the head executive of the United States.

Si **(No)** The mayor is the head executive of a state government.

Marca las respuestas para cada pregunta en la hoja que sigue. Las respuestas de esta prueba se pueden encontrat en la última página de la prueba de repaso.

1. Ⓐ Ⓑ Ⓒ Ⓓ   9. Ⓐ Ⓑ Ⓒ Ⓓ
2. Ⓐ Ⓑ Ⓒ Ⓓ   10. Ⓐ Ⓑ Ⓒ Ⓓ
3. Ⓐ Ⓑ Ⓒ Ⓓ   11. Ⓐ Ⓑ Ⓒ Ⓓ
4. Ⓐ Ⓑ Ⓒ Ⓓ   12. Ⓐ Ⓑ Ⓒ Ⓓ
5. Ⓐ Ⓑ Ⓒ Ⓓ   13. Ⓐ Ⓑ Ⓒ Ⓓ
6. Ⓐ Ⓑ Ⓒ Ⓓ   14. Ⓐ Ⓑ Ⓒ Ⓓ
7. Ⓐ Ⓑ Ⓒ Ⓓ   15. Ⓐ Ⓑ Ⓒ Ⓓ
8. Ⓐ Ⓑ Ⓒ Ⓓ

1. Who becomes President if the President and Vice President die?
   A. Congress
   B. Supreme Court justice
   C. Speaker of the House of Representatives
   D. governor

2. How many terms can a President serve?
   A. two
   B. three
   C. one
   D. no limit

3. Who becomes President of the U.S. if the President dies?
   A. Vice President
   B. Speaker of the House of Representatives
   C. mayor
   D. senator

4. What is one requirement to be President?
  A. natural born citizen of the U.S.
  B. lived in Canada
  C. be male
  D. speak Spanish

5. What special group advises the President?
  A. Congress
  B. Cabinet
  C. Parliament
  D. Supreme Court

6. Who was the first commander in chief of the U.S. military?
  A. Thomas Jefferson
  B. Bill Clinton
  C. George Bush
  D. George Washington

7. Who is commander in chief of the U.S. military?
  A. Bill Clinton
  B. George W. Bush
  C. George Washington
  D. Abraham Lincoln

8. What is the President's official home?
  A. White House
  B. New York
  C. Gray House
  D. Brown House

9. Who signs bills into law?
  A. Congress
  B. Supreme Court
  C. Vice President
  D. President

10. What is the head executive of a city government called?
  A. mayor
  B. governor
  C. President
  D. senator

11. What is the head executive of a state government called?
A. President
B. mayor
C. governor
D. Supreme Court justice

12. What is the White House?
A. where Congress meets
B. President's official home
C. governor's home
D. where Supreme Court meets

13. Where is the White House located?
A. Washington, DC
B. New York
C. Los Angeles
D. Chicago

14. In what month do we vote for President?
A. October
B. January
C. December
D. November

15. In what month is the President inaugurated?
A. March
B. April
C. September
D. January

RESPUESTAS DE LA LECCIÓN PRUEBA DE REPASO 3

1. C. Speaker of the House of Representatives
2. A. two
3. A. Vice President
4. A. natural born citizen of the U.S.
5. B. Cabinet
6. D. George Washington
7. B. George W. Bush
8. A. White House
9. D. President
10. A. mayor
11. C. governor
12. B. President's official home
13. A. Washington, DC
14. D. November
15. D. January

LECCIÓN 10

La Constitución

PALABRAS CLAVES

enmiendas: cambios

Constitución: la ley suprema de los Estados Unidos

diferente: otro

nombre de soltera: el apellido de una mujer antes de casarse.

SOBRE LA CONSTITUCIÓN

La ley suprema de los Estados Unidos es la **Constitución**. Esta comienza con la frase, "Nosotros, la gente de los Estados Unidos." La Constitución fue escrita en 1787. Puede ser cambiada. Cambios a la **Constitución** se llaman **enmiendas**. Han habido veintisiete **enmiendas** a la **Constitución**.

Constitución
- Escrita en 1787
- Empieza con "Nosotros la gente de los Estados Unidos"
- Es la ley suprema de los Estados Unidos
- Puede ser cambiada
- Los cambios se llaman enmiendas
- Tiene 27 enmiendas

LESSON 10

The Constitution

WORDS TO KNOW

amendments: changes

Constitution: the supreme law of the United States

different: other

maiden name: a woman's last name before getting married

ABOUT THE CONSTITUTION

The supreme law of the land is the **Constitution**. It begins with the words, "We the people of the United States." It was written in 1787. It can be changed. Changes to the Constitution are called **amendments**. There have been twenty-seven **amendments** to the **Constitution**.

Constitution
- Written in 1787
- Begins with "We the people of the United States"
- Is the supreme law of the United States
- Can be changed
- Changes called amendments
- Has 27 amendments

REPETICIÓN

Dí, repite, en voz alta y muchas veces estas preguntas y respuestas.

1. What is the Constitution?
the supreme law of the land

2. Can the Constitution be changed?
yes

3. What do we call changes to the Constitution?
amendments

4. How many amendments are there?
twenty-seven (27)

5. What is the supreme law of the United States?
Constitution

6. When was the Constitution written?
1787

EJERCICIOS

Los siguientes ejercicios han sido diseñados para familiarizarte con el material de esta lección. El verdadero examen de ciudadanía puede ser oral o un examen de respuestas múltiples.

Preguntas de elección múltiple

Marca tus preguntas a estas preguntas en la hoja que sigue. Las respuestas a todos los ejercicios pueden ser encontradas en la última página de esta lección.

1. Ⓐ Ⓑ Ⓒ Ⓓ   **4.** Ⓐ Ⓑ Ⓒ Ⓓ

2. Ⓐ Ⓑ Ⓒ Ⓓ   **5.** Ⓐ Ⓑ Ⓒ Ⓓ

3. Ⓐ Ⓑ Ⓒ Ⓓ

1. What is the supreme law of the land?
A. President
B. Cabinet
C. Constitution
D. Capitol

2. What is a change to the Constitution called?
A. assurance
B. amendment
C. addition
D. deletion

3. When was the Constitution written?
A. 1998
B. 1787
C. 1776
D. 1800

4. What is the Constitution?
A. the supreme law of the land
B. an award-winning book
C. the Supreme Court
D. the executive branch

5. How many amendments to the Constitution are there?
A. twenty-four
B. twenty-five
C. twenty-six
D. twenty-seven

Escribe en los espacios vacios

1. There are _____ amendments to the Constitution.
twenty-four   twenty-seven

2. A change to the Constitution is an _____.
amendment   appeal

3. The Constitution is the supreme _____ of the land.
law   crime

4. _____, the Constitution can be changed.
No   Yes

5. The supreme law of the land is the _____.
Constitution   Congress

6. The Constitution was written in _____.
1787   1785

Preguntas de Si o No

Encierra **Si** en un círculo si la oración es correcta. Encierra **No** si la oración no es correcta.

Si	No	The Constitution is the supreme law of the land.
Si	No	A change to the Constitution is called an amendment.
Si	No	The Constitution cannot be changed.
Si	No	The Constitution was written in 1776.
Si	No	The supreme law of the land is the Constitution.
Si	No	There are twenty-seven amendments to the Constitution.
Si	No	The Constitution was written in 1787.
Si	No	There are twenty-four amendments to the Constitution.

PRACTICA DE DICTADO

Escribe cada oración dos veces. La primera vez, copia la lección. La segunda vez, haz que alguien lea la oración mientras la escribes.

1. The sky is blue.

2. My dog is brown.

3. The sky is blue and my dog is brown.

1. _____.

1. _____.

2. _____.

2. _____.

3. _____.

3. _____.

PRACTICA PARA LA ENTREVISTA

Di, repite, en voz alta y muchas veces estas preguntas y respuestas.

Pregunta: Have you ever used a different name?
Respuesta: Yes, my last name used to be Alloutuseth.

Pregunta: Do you want to change your name?
Respuesta: Yes, I want to change my last name to Allseth.

Pregunta: What other names have you gone by?
Respuesta: I used to be called Massouleh Alloutuseth.

Pregunta: To what do you want to change your name?
Respuesta: I want my new name to be Sue Allseth.

Pregunta: What name do you want to have now?
Respuesta: Sue Allseth.

Pregunta: How do you spell that?
Respuesta: S-u-e A-l-l-s-e-t-h.

Pregunta: What other names have you used in the past?
Respuesta: I've never used any other names.

Pregunta: What was your maiden name?
Respuesta: Before I was married, my name was Massouleh Tomei.

Pregunta: What other names have you used in the past?
Respuesta: Before I was married my name was Massouleh Tomei.

Pregunta: When did you change your name?
Respuesta: I changed my name ten years ago when I was married.

Tu Turno

Haz que alguien te haga las preguntas anteriores. Responde con las preguntas que sean para tí correctas.

RESPUESTAS DE LA LECCIÓN 10

Preguntas de elección múltiple
1. C. Constitution
2. B. amendment
3. B. 1787
4. A. the supreme law of the land
5. D. twenty-seven

Escribe en los espacios vacios
1. There are <u>twenty-seven</u> amendments to the Constitution.
2. A change to the Constitution is an <u>amendment</u>.
3. The Constitution is the supreme <u>law</u> of the land.
4. <u>Yes</u>, the Constitution can be changed.
5. The supreme law of the land is the <u>Constitution</u>.
6. The Constitution was written in <u>1787</u>.

Preguntas de Si o No

(Si)   No   The Constitution is the supreme law of the land.

(Si)   No   A change to the Constitution is called an amendment.

Si   (No)   The Constitution cannot be changed.

Si   (No)   The Constitution was written in 1776.

(Si)   No   The supreme law of the land is the Constitution.

(Si)   No   There are twenty-seven amendments to the Constitution.

(Si)   No   The Constitution was written in 1787.

Si   (No)   There are twenty-four amendments to the Constitution.

LECCIÓN 11

Más sobre la Constitución

PALABRAS CLAVES

arrestado: formalmente acusado por un oficial de policía

crimen: rompimiento de la ley

introducción: el principio

preámbulo: la introducción a la constitución

ley suprema: la ley más importante, la más alta

SOBRE LA CONSTITUCION

La Constitución es la **ley suprema** del país. La **introducción** de la Constitución es conocida como el **preámbulo**. Las primeras diez enmiendas a la Constitución son llamadas Declaración de los Derechos. Una de estas enmiendas dentro de la Declaración de los Derechos permite el derecho a la palabra. Todas las personas en los Estados Unidos, incluyendo a los no-ciudadanos, estan protegidas por la Constitución y el Declaración de los Derechos.

Constitución
- Tiene una introducción llamada preámbulo
- Es la ley suprema del país
- Proteje a todos dentro de los Estados Unidos, incluyendo no-ciudadanos

Declaración de los Derechos
- Las primeras diez enmiendas a la Constitución
- Ofrece el derecho a la palabra
- Proteje a todos en los Estados Unidos, incluyendo no-ciudadanos

Turn page for English translation

LESSON 11

More about the Constitution

WORDS TO KNOW

arrested: formally charged by a police officer

crime: breaking the law

introduction: the beginning

preamble: the introduction to the Constitution

supreme law: the highest, most important law

ABOUT THE CONSTITUTION

The Constitution is the **supreme law** of the land. The **introduction** to the Constitution is called the **preamble**. The first ten amendments to the Constitution are called the Bill of Rights. One of the amendments in the Bill of Rights grants freedom of speech. Everyone in the United States is protected by the Constitution and the Bill of Rights, including non-citizens.

Constitution
- Has **introduction** called **preamble**
- Is **supreme law** of the land
- Protects everyone in the United States, including non-citizens

Bill of Rights
- The first ten amendments to the Constitution
- Grants freedom of speech
- Protects everyone in the United States, including non-citizens

---

REPETICIÓN

Di, repite, en voz alta y muchas veces estas preguntas y respuestas.

1. **What is the Bill of Rights?**
   the first ten amendments

2. **Where does the freedom of speech come from?**
   the Bill of Rights

3. **What are the first ten amendments called?**
   the Bill of Rights

4. **Whose rights are guaranteed by the Constitution and the Bill of Rights?**
   everyone in the United States, including non-citizens

5. **What is the introduction to the Constitution called?**
   the preamble

EJERCICIOS

Los siguientes ejercicios han sido diseñados para familiarizarte con el material de esta lección. El verdadero examen de ciudadanía puede ser oral o un examen de respuestas múltiples.

Preguntas de elección múltiple

Marca tus preguntas a estas preguntas en la hoja que sigue. Las respuestas a todos los ejercicios pueden ser encontradas en la última página de esta lección.

1. Ⓐ Ⓑ Ⓒ Ⓓ   4. Ⓐ Ⓑ Ⓒ Ⓓ
2. Ⓐ Ⓑ Ⓒ Ⓓ   5. Ⓐ Ⓑ Ⓒ Ⓓ
3. Ⓐ Ⓑ Ⓒ Ⓓ

1. **What are the first ten amendments to the Constitution called?**
   A. preamble
   B. introduction
   C. Bill of Rights
   D. Book of Law

2. What is the Bill of Rights?
   A. last ten amendments to the Constitution
   B. changes to the Declaration of Statehood
   C. additions to the President's speech
   D. first ten amendments to the Constitution

3. Where does freedom of speech come from?
   A. Bill of Rights
   B. President
   C. Pilgrims
   D. Supreme Court

4. Whose rights are guaranteed by the Constitution?
   A. Canadians
   B. Europeans
   C. American citizens only
   D. everyone in the United States, including non-citizens

5. What is the introduction to the Constitution called?
   A. preamble
   B. epilogue
   C. beginning
   D. story

Encierra en un círculo la respuesta correcta.

1. the first ten amendments
   Bill of Rights   Congress

2. the introduction to the Constitution
   preamble   Bill of Rights

3. freedom of speech comes from here
   President   Bill of Rights

4. the Constitution guarantees these people rights
   everyone   only citizens

5. the Bill of Rights
   first ten amendments   Supreme Court

Preguntas de Si o No

Encierra **Si** en un círculo si la oración es correcta. Encierra **No** si la oración no es correcta.

Si	No	The Constitution is the supreme law of the land.
Si	No	The first ten amendments to the Constitution are called the Bill of Rights.
Si	No	Freedom of speech comes from the Bill of Rights.
Si	No	The Bill of Rights is the first twelve amendments to the Constitution.
Si	No	The introduction to the Constitution is called the preamble.
Si	No	Everyone is protected by the Bill of Rights, including non-citizens.
Si	No	The Bill of Rights is the first ten amendments to the Constitution.
Si	No	The conclusion to the Constitution is called the preamble.

PRACTICA DE DICTADO

Escribe cada oración dos veces. La primera vez, copia la lección. La segunda vez, haz que alguien lea la oración mientras la escribes.

1. There is a bird.

2. The bird is in the tree.

3. There is a bird in the tree.

1. _____.

1. _____.

2. _____.

2. _____.

3. _____.

3. _____.

Di, repite, en voz alta y muchas veces estas preguntas y respuestas.

Pregunta: Why do you want to be an American citizen?
Respuesta: I want to vote.

Pregunta: Why do you want to be a U.S. citizen?
Respuesta: I want to travel with a U.S. passport.

Pregunta: Why have you applied for naturalization?
Respuesta: I want to bring my mother to the United States.

Pregunta: Were you ever arrested?
Respuesta: Yes, a long time ago.

Pregunta: What were you arrested for?
Respuesta: I stole some money from the corner store.

Pregunta: How about any other arrests?
Respuesta: No, that was the only time I was arrested.

Pregunta: Have you ever committed any crime for which you have not been arrested?
Respuesta: No, I've never done any crimes that I wasn't punished for.

Pregunta: Have you ever been imprisoned for breaking any law?
Respuesta: I was in jail for three months for robbing the corner store.

Pregunta: When was that?
Respuesta: During the winter of 1989.

Tu Turno

Haz que alguien te haga las preguntas anteriores. Responde con las preguntas que sean para tí correctas.

RESPUESTAS DE LA LECCIÓN 11

Preguntas de elección múltiple
1. C. Bill of Rights
2. D. first ten amendments to the Constitution
3. A. Bill of Rights
4. D. everyone in the United States, including non-citizens
5. A. preamble

Encierra en un círculo la respuesta correcta.
1. the first ten amendments
   (Bill of Rights)   Congress

2. the introduction to the Constitution
   (preamble)   Bill of Rights

3. freedom of speech comes from here
   President   (Bill of Rights)

4. the Constitution guarantees these people rights
   (everyone)   only citizens

5. the Bill of Rights
   (first ten amendments)   Supreme Court

Preguntas de Si o No

(Si)   No   The Constitution is the supreme law of the land.

(Si)   No   The first ten amendments to the Constitution are called the Bill of Rights.

(Si)   No   Freedom of speech comes from the Bill of Rights.

Si   (No)   The Bill of Rights is the first twelve amendments to the Constitution.

(Si)   No   The introduction to the Constitution is called the preamble.

(Si)   No   Everyone is protected by the Bill of Rights, including non-citizens.

(Si)   No   The Bill of Rights is the first ten amendments to the Constitution.

Si   (No)   The conclusion to the Constitution is called the preamble.

LECCIÓN 12

Declaración de los Derechos

PALABRAS CLAVES

portar armas: llevar una pistola

Declaración de los Derechos: primeras diez enmiendas

impuestos de ganancia: el dinero que pagas al gobierno si trabajas en los Estados Unidos

juzgado: puesto en juicio delante de un juez y un jurado

autorización: permiso oficial del juez

SOBRE LA DECLARACIÓN DE LOS DERECHOS

La Constitución es la ley suprema del país. Las primeras diez enmiendas a la Constitución son llamadas **La Declaración de los Derechos**. Todos en los Estados Unidos están protegidos por la **Declaración de los Derechos**, inclusive los no-ciudadanos. Algunos puntos de la **Declaración de los Derechos** son:

- La libertad de expresión, prensa, y religión.
- Libertad de **portar armas**
- El gobierno no puede poner soldados en las casas de la gente
- El gobierno no puede buscar o tomar posesión de las propiedades de una persona sin tener una **autorización**.
- Una persona no puede ser **juzgada** dos veces por el mismo crimen
- Una persona acusada de un crimen tiene el derecho a un abogado y a un juicio
- La gente está protegida en contra de multas irrazonables o castigos crueles.

LESSON 12

Bill of Rights

WORDS TO KNOW

bear arms:	carry a gun
Bill of Rights:	first ten amendments
income tax:	the money you pay to the government if you work in the United States
tried:	put through a trial with a judge and jury
warrant:	official permission from a judge

ABOUT THE BILL OF RIGHTS

The Constitution is the supreme law of the land. The first ten amendments to the Constitution are called the **Bill of Rights**. Everyone in the United States is protected by the **Bill of Rights**, including non-citizens. Some of the **Bill of Rights** include:

- The freedom of speech, press, and religion
- Right to **bear arms**
- Government may not put soldiers in people's homes
- Government may not search or take a person's property without a **warrant**
- A person may not be **tried** for the same crime twice
- A person charged with a crime has rights including the right to a trial and a lawyer
- People are protected from unreasonable fines or cruel punishment

REPETICIÓN

Di, repite, en voz alta y muchas veces estas preguntas y respuestas.

1. What are the first ten amendments?
Bill of Rights

2. What are the freedoms guaranteed by the Bill of Rights?
- The freedom of speech, press, and religion
- Right to bear arms
- Government may not put soldiers in people's homes
- Government may not search or take a person's property without a warrant
- A person may not be tried for the same crime twice
- A person charged with a crime has rights including the right to a trial and a lawyer
- People are protected from unreasonable fines or cruel punishment

3. Name one right guaranteed by the First Amendment.
freedom of: speech, press, religion, peaceable assembly, and change of government

EJERCICIOS

Los siguientes ejercicios han sido diseñados para familiarizarte con el material de esta lección. El verdadero examen de ciudadanía puede ser oral o un examen de respuestas múltiples.

Multiple Choice Questions
Marca tus preguntas a estas preguntas en la hoja que sigue. Las respuestas a todos los ejercicios pueden ser encontradas en la última página de esta lección.

1. Ⓐ Ⓑ Ⓒ Ⓓ   **4.** Ⓐ Ⓑ Ⓒ Ⓓ
2. Ⓐ Ⓑ Ⓒ Ⓓ   **5.** Ⓐ Ⓑ Ⓒ Ⓓ
3. Ⓐ Ⓑ Ⓒ Ⓓ

1. What are the first ten amendments to the Constitution called?
A. preamble
B. introduction
C. Bill of Rights
D. Book of Law

2. Which freedom is guaranteed by the Bill of Rights?
   A. right to pay taxes
   B. right to bear arms
   C. right to get paid for your work
   D. right to govern your neighbor

3. Which freedom is guaranteed by the Bill of Rights?
   A. government may put soldiers in people's homes
   B. government may search anyone without a warrant
   C. government may not enter contests
   D. government may not put soldiers in people's homes

4. Which freedom is guaranteed by the Bill of Rights?
   A. a person may not be tried for the same crime twice
   B. a person may walk on the moon
   C. a person may kill his or her neighbor
   D. a person charged with a crime may not get a trial

5. Which freedom is guaranteed by the Bill of Rights?
   A. freedom to steal from your neighbor
   B. freedom of speech
   C. freedom to fight the government
   D. freedom to set off a bomb

Preguntas cortas

What are the freedoms guaranteed by the Bill of Rights?

1. _____.

2. _____.

3. _____.

4. _____.

5. _____.

6. _____.

7. _____.

Preguntas de Si o No

Encierra **Si** en un círculo si la oración es correcta. Encierra **No** si la oración no es correcta.

Si	No	The Constitution is the supreme law of the land.
Si	No	The first ten amendments to the Constitution are called the Bill of Rights.
Si	No	Freedom of speech comes from the Bill of Rights.
Si	No	The right to bear arms comes from the Bill of Rights.
Si	No	Everyone is protected by the Bill of Rights, including non-citizens.
Si	No	The government may not search or take a person's property without a warrant.
Si	No	The Bill of Rights is the first ten amendments to the Constitution.
Si	No	A person in the United States may not be tried for the same crime twice.
Si	No	People in the United States are not protected from unreasonable fines.
Si	No	Freedom of religion comes from the Bill of Rights.
Si	No	The government may not put soldiers in people's homes.

PRACTICA DE DICTADO

Escribe cada oración dos veces. La primera vez, copia la lección. La segunda vez, haz que alguien lea la oración mientras la escribes.

1. I have four children.

2. I live with my children.

3. I live with my four children.

1. _____.

1. _____.

2. _____.

2. _____.

3. _____ ★.

3. _____.

PRACTICA PARA LA ENTREVISTA

Di, repite, en voz alta y muchas veces estas preguntas y respuestas.

Pregunta: Have you ever failed to file a federal income tax return?
Respuesta: No, I have always filed my taxes.

Pregunta: Have you filed your federal taxes every year?
Respuesta: Yes, I pay my taxes every year.

Pregunta: Do you pay taxes?
Respuesta: Yes, I pay federal and state taxes each year.

Pregunta: Was there ever a year when you didn't file your federal tax forms?
Respuesta: No, I've filed my tax forms every year since I came to the United States.

Pregunta: Was there ever a year when you didn't file your federal tax forms?
Respuesta: Yes, I didn't file my first two years in the United States because I made no money.

Pregunta: Do you pay taxes?
Respuesta: No, I don't have a job so I don't pay federal income taxes.

Tu Turno

Haz que alguien te haga las preguntas anteriores. Responde con las preguntas que sean para tí correctas.

RESPUESTAS DE LA LECCIÓN 12

Preguntas de elección múltiple
1. C. Bill of Rights
2. B. right to bear arms
3. D. government may not put soldiers in people's homes
4. A. a person may not be tried for the same crime twice
5. B. freedom of speech

Preguntas cortas
1. The freedom of speech, press, and religion
2. Right to bear arms
3. Government may not put soldiers in people's homes
4. Government may not search or take a person's property without a warrant
5. A person may not be tried for the same crime twice
6. A person charged with a crime has rights including the right to a trial and a lawyer
7. People are protected from unreasonable fines or cruel punishment

Preguntas de Si o No

Encierra **Si** en un círculo si la oración es correcta. Encierra **No** si la oración no es correcta.

(Si)   No   The Constitution is the supreme law of the land.

(Si)   No   The first ten amendments to the Constitution are called the Bill of Rights.

(Si)   No   Freedom of speech comes from the Bill of Rights.

(Si)   No   The right to bear arms comes from the Bill of Rights.

(Si)   No   Everyone is protected by the Bill of Rights, including non-citizens.

(Si)   No   The government may not search or take a person's property without a warrant.

(Si)   No   The Bill of Rights is the first ten amendments to the Constitution.

(Si)   No   A person in the United States may not be tried for the same crime twice.

Si (No) People in the United States are not protected from unreasonable fines.

(Si) No Freedom of religion comes from the Bill of Rights.

(Si) No The government may not put soldiers in people's homes.

PRUEBA DE REPASO 4

Marca las respuestas para cada pregunta en la hoja que sigue. Las respuestas de esta prueba se pueden encontrar en la última página de la prueba de repaso.

1. Ⓐ Ⓑ Ⓒ Ⓓ   7. Ⓐ Ⓑ Ⓒ Ⓓ
2. Ⓐ Ⓑ Ⓒ Ⓓ   8. Ⓐ Ⓑ Ⓒ Ⓓ
3. Ⓐ Ⓑ Ⓒ Ⓓ   9. Ⓐ Ⓑ Ⓒ Ⓓ
4. Ⓐ Ⓑ Ⓒ Ⓓ   10. Ⓐ Ⓑ Ⓒ Ⓓ
5. Ⓐ Ⓑ Ⓒ Ⓓ   11. Ⓐ Ⓑ Ⓒ Ⓓ
6. Ⓐ Ⓑ Ⓒ Ⓓ   12. Ⓐ Ⓑ Ⓒ Ⓓ

1. When was the Constitution written?
   A. 1787
   B. 1789
   C. 1777
   D. 1749

2. What is the supreme law of the United States?
   A. Declaration of Independence
   B. Constitution
   C. Supreme Court
   D. Congress

3. How many amendments are there?
   A. twenty-three
   B. twenty-five
   C. twenty-six
   D. twenty-seven

4. What do we call a change to the Constitution?
   A. amendment
   B. objection
   C. law
   D. President

5. Can the Constitution be changed?
   A. no
   B. yes

6. What is the Constitution?
   A. supreme law of the land
   B. Congress
   C. Supreme Court
   D. Declaration of Independence

7. What are the first ten amendments called?
   A. supreme law
   B. Constitution
   C. Bill of Rights
   D. citizen rights

8. Whose rights are guaranteed by the Constitution?
   A. only citizens
   B. only the President
   C. only Congress
   D. both citizens and non-citizens

9. What is the introduction to the Constitution called?
   A. Bill of Rights
   B. supreme law of the land
   C. preface
   D. preamble

10. Where does the freedom of speech come from?
   A. President
   B. Congress
   C. Bill of Rights
   D. Supreme Court

11. What is the Bill of Rights?
   A. first ten amendments
   B. Declaration of Independence
   C. code of ethics
   D. code of good works

12. What is one right guaranteed by the Bill of Rights?
   A. freedom of speech
   B. freedom to fight the government
   C. freedom to kill your neighbor
   D. freedom to rob your neighbor

RESPUESTAS DE LA LECCIÓN PRUEBA DE REPASO 4

1. A. 1787
2. B. Constitution
3. D. twenty-seven
4. A. amendment
5. B. yes
6. A. supreme law of the land
7. C. Bill of Rights
8. D. both citizens and non-citizens
9. D. preamble
10. C. Bill of Rights
11. A. first ten amendments
12. A. freedom of speech

LECCIÓN 13

Peregrinos

PALABRAS CLAVES

enbriagado:	persona que toma mucha alcohol
Indígenas Americanos:	gente que vivía en América cuando los peregrinos llegaron
peregrinos (pilgrims):	gente que vino a América en un barco llamado Mayflower
poligamia:	tener más de un esposo o esposa al mismo tiempo
prostituta:	persona que vende su cuerpo por dinero
Día de acción de gracia:	un feriado que fue en principio celebrado por los peregrinos y los indígenas americanos.

SOBRE LOS PEREGRINOS

Los peregrinos vinieron a América buscando libertad religiosa. **Los peregrinos** fueron los primeros colonizadores americanos. Cuando llegaron a América, se encontraron con los Indígenas Americanos. **Los Indígenas Americanos** ayudaron a los peregrinos. **Los peregrinos** vinieron a América en un barco llamado el Mayflower. En América, el primer feriado que **los peregrinos** celebraron fue el día de acción de gracia. Ellos lo celebraron con **los Indígenas Americanos.**

Peregrinos
- Llegaron en el Mayflower
- Fueron los primeros colonizadores
- Vinieron por libertad religiosa
- Conocieron y recibieron ayuda de los Indígenas Americanos
- Celebraron el primer feriado, el día de acción de gracia

Turn page for English translation

LESSON 13

Pilgrims

WORDS TO KNOW

habitual drunkard: person who drinks too much alcohol

Native Americans: people who lived in America when the pilgrims arrived

Pilgrims: people who came to America on a ship called the Mayflower

polygamy: having more than one husband or one wife at the same time

prostitute: to sell your body for money

Thanksgiving: a holiday that was first celebrated by the pilgrims and the Native Americans

ABOUT THE PILGRIMS

The **Pilgrims** came to America for religious freedom. The **Pilgrims** were the first American colonists. When they came to America, they met the **Native Americans**. The **Native Americans** helped the **Pilgrims**. The **Pilgrims** came to America on a ship called the Mayflower. In America, the first holiday the **Pilgrims** celebrated was **Thanksgiving**. They celebrated it with the **Native Americans**.

Pilgrims
- Arrive on the Mayflower
- Were first colonists
- Came for religious freedom
- Met and got help from Native Americans
- Celebrated the first Thanksgiving

REPETICIÓN

Di, repite, en voz alta y muchas veces estas preguntas y respuestas.

1. **Why did the Pilgrims come to America?**
   religious freedom

2. **Who helped the Pilgrims in America?**
   Native Americans

3. **What ship brought the Pilgrims to America?**
   Mayflower

4. **What holiday was celebrated for the first time by the American colonists?**
   Thanksgiving

5. **Who were the first American colonists?**
   Pilgrims

EJERCICIOS

Los siguientes ejercicios han sido diseñados para familiarizarte con el material de esta lección. El verdadero examen de ciudadanía puede ser oral o un examen de respuestas múltiples.

Preguntas de elección múltiple

Marca tus preguntas a estas preguntas en la hoja que sigue. Las respuestas a todos los ejercicios pueden ser encontradas en la última página de esta lección.

1. (A) (B) (C) (D)   4. (A) (B) (C) (D)
2. (A) (B) (C) (D)   5. (A) (B) (C) (D)
3. (A) (B) (C) (D)

1. **Who did the Pilgrims meet when they came to America?**
   A. Native Americans
   B. Europeans
   C. Canadians
   D. judges

---

2. Why did the Pilgrims come to America?
   A. chance to get rich
   B. hope for new homes
   C. religious freedom
   D. to leave their relatives

3. What ship brought the Pilgrims to America?
   A. Red Rose
   B. Mayday
   C. Flower
   D. Mayflower

4. What holiday did the Pilgrims celebrate with the Native Americans?
   A. Thanksgiving
   B. Halloween
   C. Easter
   D. Valentine's Day

5. Who helped the Pilgrims when they arrived in America?
   A. animals
   B. Native Americans
   C. Mexicans
   D. Chinese

Preguntas para agrupar
Responde cada pregunta con la respuesta más apropiada.

_____ ship that brought the Pilgrims to America
_____ helped the Pilgrims in America
_____ holiday celebrated by the American colonists
_____ reason pilgrims came to America

A. Thanksgiving
B. religious freedom
C. Native Americans
D. *Mayflower*

Preguntas de Si o No
Encierra **Si** en un círculo si la oración es correcta. Encierra **No** si la oración no es correcta.

Si   No   The Native Americans helped the Pilgrims.

Si   No   The Pilgrims came to America because they wanted a vacation.

Si   No   The Pilgrims came to America on a ship called the *Titanic*.

Si   No   Thanksgiving was the first holiday celebrated by the Pilgrims.

Si	No	The Pilgrims were the first American colonists.
Si	No	The Pilgrims came to America for religious freedom.
Si	No	Easter was the first holiday celebrated by the Pilgrims.
Si	No	A ship called the *Mayflower* brought the Pilgrims to America.

PRACTICA DE DICTADO

Escribe cada oración dos veces. La primera vez, copia la lección. La segunda vez, haz que alguien lea la oración mientras la escribes.

1. I drive a car.

2. I drive a big red car.

3. I like my car.

1. _____.

1. _____.

2. _____.

2. _____.

3. _____.

3. _____.

PRACTICA PARA LA ENTREVISTA

Di, repite, en voz alta y muchas veces estas preguntas y respuestas.

Pregunta:	Have you ever been a habitual drunkard?
Respuesta:	No, I don't drink alcohol.

Pregunta:	Have you ever been a habitual drunkard?
Respuesta:	No, I drink only a little.

Pregunta:	Were you ever drunk every day?
Respuesta:	No, I drink only one glass of wine a week.

Pregunta:	Have you ever advocated or practiced polygamy?
Respuesta:	No, I have only one wife.
Pregunta:	Have you ever been married to more than one person at a time?
Respuesta:	No, I have always had only one husband.
Pregunta:	Have you ever practiced polygamy?
Respuesta:	No, I am not married, and I have never been married.
Pregunta:	Have you ever been a prostitute?
Respuesta:	No, I don't sell my body.
Pregunta:	Have you ever been a prostitute?
Respuesta:	No, I've never taken money for sex.
Pregunta:	Have you ever sold your body for money?
Respuesta:	No, I've never been a prostitute.

Tu Turno

Haz que alguien te haga las preguntas anteriores. Responde con las preguntas que sean para tí correctas.

RESPUESTAS DE LA LECCIÓN 13

Preguntas de elección múltiple

1. A. Native Americans
2. C. religious freedom
3. D. Mayflower
4. A. Thanksgiving
5. B. Native Americans

Matching Answers

  D   ship that brought the pilgrims to America   A. Thanksgiving
  C   helped the pilgrims in America   B. religious freedom
  A   holiday celebrated by the American   C. Native Americans
      colonists   D. *Mayflower*
  B   reason pilgrims came to America

Preguntas de Si o No

(Si)   No   The Native Americans helped the Pilgrims.

Si   **(No)**   The Pilgrims came to America because they wanted a vacation.

Si   **(No)**   The Pilgrims came to America on a ship called the *Titanic*.

(Si)   No   Thanksgiving was the first holiday celebrated by the Pilgrims.

(Si)   No   The Pilgrims were the first American colonists.

(Si)   No   The Pilgrims came to America for religious freedom.

Si   **(No)**   Easter was the first holiday celebrated by the Pilgrims.

(Si)   No   A ship called the *Mayflower* brought the Pilgrims to America.

LECCIÓN 14

Colonias

PALABRAS CLAVES

colonias: los primeros trece estados de América

drogas ilegales: narcóticos, cocaína, marijuana, estupefacientes

apuesta ilegal: jugar a las cartas por dinero

contrabando: hacer pasar ilegalmente al país algo o alguien

SOBRE LAS COLONIAS

Originalmente, los primeros estados se llamaban **colonias.** Las primeras trece **colonias** eran Connecticut, New Hampshire, New York, New Jersey, Massachusetts, Pennsylvania, Delaware, Virginia, North Carolina, South Carolina, Georgia, Rhode Island, and Maryland. Las **colonias** eran gobernadas por el rey de Inglaterra, el Rey George.

Colonias (gobernadas por el rey George)

Connecticut	New York
Delaware	North Carolina
Georgia	Pennsylvania
Maryland	Rhode Island
Massachusetts	South Carolina
New Hampshire	Virginia
New Jersey	

LESSON 14

Colonies

WORDS TO KNOW

colonies: original thirteen states in America

illegal drugs: narcotics, cocaine, marijuana, dope, speed

illegal gambling: to play cards for money

smuggle: illegally sneaking someone or something into the country

ABOUT THE COLONIES

The thirteen original states were called the **colonies**. The original thirteen **colonies** were Connecticut, New Hampshire, New York, New Jersey, Massachusetts, Pennsylvania, Delaware, Virginia, North Carolina, South Carolina, Georgia, Rhode Island, and Maryland. The **colonies** were ruled by the king of England, King George.

Colonies (ruled by King George)

Connecticut	New York
Delaware	North Carolina
Georgia	Pennsylvania
Maryland	Rhode Island
Massachusetts	South Carolina
New Hampshire	Virginia
New Jersey	

REPETICIÓN

Di, repite, en voz alta y muchas veces estas preguntas y respuestas.

1. What are the thirteen original states called?   colonies

2. Can you name the original thirteen states?
- Connecticut
- Delaware
- Georgia
- Maryland
- Massachusetts
- New Hampshire
- New Jersey
- New York
- North Carolina
- Pennsylvania
- Rhode Island
- South Carolina
- Virginia

EJERCICIOS

Los siguientes ejercicios han sido diseñados para familiarizarte con el material de esta lección. El verdadero examen de ciudadanía puede ser oral o un examen de respuestas múltiples.

Preguntas de elección múltiple

Marca tus preguntas a estas preguntas en la hoja que sigue. Las respuestas a todos los ejercicios pueden ser encontradas en la última página de esta lección.

1. Ⓐ Ⓑ Ⓒ Ⓓ   **4.** Ⓐ Ⓑ Ⓒ Ⓓ

2. Ⓐ Ⓑ Ⓒ Ⓓ   **5.** Ⓐ Ⓑ Ⓒ Ⓓ

3. Ⓐ Ⓑ Ⓒ Ⓓ

1. What were the thirteen original states called?
A. Native American cities
B. colonies
C. states
D. settlements

2. Which state was a part of the thirteen colonies?
   A. Connecticut
   B. California
   C. Washington
   D. Nevada

3. Which state was a part of the thirteen colonies?
   A. Texas
   B. New York
   C. California
   D. Minnesota

4. Which state was a part of the thirteen colonies?
   A. Virginia
   B. California
   C. Texas
   D. Oregon

5. Which state was a part of the thirteen colonies?
   A. Maryland
   B. California
   C. Wisconsin
   D. Texas

Escribe en los espacios vacios

1. The original thirteen states were called the _____.
   colonies   provinces

2. Name two of the original thirteen states: _____ and _____.
   Connecticut/New Hampshire   Texas/Maine

3. Name two more of the original thirteen states: _____ and _____.
   California/Utah   New York/New Jersey

Preguntas de Si o No

Encierra **Si** en un círculo si la oración es correcta. Encierra **No** si la oración no es correcta.

| Si | No | The thirteen original states were called the colonies. |

| Si | No | New York was one of the colonies. |

| Si | No | Texas was one of the colonies. |

| Si | No | The thirteen original states were called the settlements. |

Si   No   Connecticut was one of the original thirteen states.

Si   No   California was one of the original thirteen states.

Si   No   Georgia was one of the colonies.

Si   No   Maryland was one of the original thirteen states.

PRACTICA DE DICTADO

Escribe cada oración dos veces. La primera vez, copia la lección. La segunda vez, haz que alguien lea la oración mientras la escribes.

1. I live in a house.

2. I live in a blue house.

3. I like my house.

1. _____.

1. _____.

2. _____.

2. _____.

3. _____.

3. _____.

PRACTICA PARA LA ENTREVISTA

Di, repite, en voz alta y muchas veces estas preguntas y respuestas.

Pregunta:	Have you ever knowingly and for gain helped any alien to enter the U.S. illegally?
Respuesta:	No, I have never smuggled anyone into the country.
Pregunta:	Have you ever helped someone enter the U.S. illegally?
Respuesta:	No, I have never smuggled anyone into the country.
Pregunta:	Have you ever smuggled anyone into the U.S.?
Respuesta:	No, I have never helped anyone enter the United States illegally.

Pregunta:	Have you ever accepted money for sneaking someone into the U.S.?
Respuesta:	No, I have never helped anyone enter the United States illegally.
Pregunta:	Have you ever been a trafficker in illegal drugs?
Respuesta:	No, I have never touched illegal drugs.
Pregunta:	Have you ever bought or sold illegal drugs?
Respuesta:	No, I have never purchased or sold illegal drugs.
Pregunta:	Have you ever carried illegal drugs for someone else?
Respuesta:	No, I have never handled illegal drugs.
Pregunta:	Have you ever been a trafficker of illegal drugs?
Respuesta:	No, I have never sold or carried drugs.
Pregunta:	Have you ever received income from illegal gambling?
Respuesta:	No, I don't gamble.
Pregunta:	Did you ever get money illegally from gambling?
Respuesta:	No, I don't gamble for money.
Pregunta:	Have you ever received money from illegal gambling?
Respuesta:	No, I don't gamble for money.
Pregunta:	Have you ever received money or other goods from illegal gambling?
Respuesta:	No, I don't bet on anything.

Tu Turno

Haz que alguien te haga las preguntas anteriores. Responde con las preguntas que sean para tí correctas.

RESPUESTAS DE LA LECCIÓN 14

Preguntas de elección múltiple
1. B. colonies
2. A. Connecticut
3. B. New York
4. A. Virginia
5. A. Maryland

Escribe en los espacios vacios
The original thirteen states were called the <u>colonies</u>.
Name two of the original thirteen states: <u>Connecticut</u> and <u>New Hampshire</u>.
Name two more of the original thirteen states: <u>New York</u> and <u>New Jersey</u>.

Preguntas de Si o No

(Si)   No   The thirteen original states were called the colonies.

(Si)   No   New York was one of the colonies.

Si   (No)   Texas was one of the colonies.

Si   (No)   The thirteen original states were called the settlements.

(Si)   No   Connecticut was one of the original thirteen states.

Si   (No)   California was one of the original thirteen states.

(Si)   No   Georgia was one of the colonies.

(Si)   No   Maryland was one of the original thirteen states.

LECCIÓN 15

La Declaración de la Independencia

PALABRAS CLAVES

adoptado: poner en efecto

creencia fundamental: idea principal, parte más importante

aclamado: decir algo cierto; pretendido

Declaración de Independencia: documento escrito que dice que las colonias querían ser liberadas de Inglaterra.

Día de la Independencia: 4 de Julio

registrado: oficialmente apuntado a hacer algo

SOBRE LAS COLONIAS

Las colonias no estaban contentas que Inglaterra las gobernara. Entonces, Thomas Jefferson escribió la **Declaración de Independencia.** La Declaración dice que las colonias querían ser liberadas de Inglaterra. La **creeencia fundamental** es que todos los hombres han sido creados igualmente. La **Declaración de Independencia** fue **adoptada** el 4 de Julio de 1776. En los Estados Unidos, el 4 de Julio es el **Día de la Independencia.**

Declaración de Independencia
- Escrita por Thomas Jefferson
- Declara que todos los hombres han sido creados igualmente
- Declara que las colonias querían ser libres de Inglaterra
- Adoptada el 4 de Julio de 1776

Turn page for English translation

LESSON 15

 *Declaration of Independence*

WORDS TO KNOW

adopted: put into effect

basic belief: main idea, most important part

claimed: said something was true; pretended

Declaration of Independence: written statement saying the colonies wanted to be free from England

Independence Day: July 4th

registered: officially signed up to do something

ABOUT THE COLONIES

The colonies were not happy being ruled by England. So Thomas Jefferson wrote the **Declaration of Independence**. The Declaration said that the colonies wanted to be free from England. The **basic belief** of the **Declaration of Independence** is that all men are created equal. The **Declaration of Independence** was **adopted** on July 4, 1776. July 4th in the United States is **Independence Day**.

Declaration of Independence
- Written by Thomas Jefferson
- States all men are created equal
- Stated that the colonies wanted to be free of England
- Adopted on July 4, 1776

REPETICIÓN

Di, repite, en voz alta y muchas veces estas preguntas y respuestas.

1. What is the 4th of July?
   Independence Day

2. When was the Declaration of Independence adopted?
   July 4, 1776

3. What is the basic belief of the Declaration of Independence?
   All men are created equal.

4. Who was the main writer of the Declaration of Independence?
   Thomas Jefferson

5. What is the date of Independence Day?
   July 4th

EJERCICIOS

Los siguientes ejercicios han sido diseñados para familiarizarte con el material de esta lección. El verdadero examen de ciudadanía puede ser oral o un examen de respuestas múltiples.

Preguntas de elección múltiple

Marca tus preguntas a estas preguntas en la hoja que sigue. Las respuestas a todos los ejercicios pueden ser encontradas en la última página de esta lección.

1. Ⓐ Ⓑ Ⓒ Ⓓ   4. Ⓐ Ⓑ Ⓒ Ⓓ
2. Ⓐ Ⓑ Ⓒ Ⓓ   5. Ⓐ Ⓑ Ⓒ Ⓓ
3. Ⓐ Ⓑ Ⓒ Ⓓ

1. When was the Declaration of Independence adopted?
   A. 1776
   B. 1777
   C. 1789
   D. 1787

---

2. What is the basic belief of the Declaration of Independence?
   A. all men should fight in an army
   B. all men are created equal
   C. the President has absolute power
   D. only citizens can live in America

3. Who was the main writer of the Declaration of Independence?
   A. Abraham Lincoln
   B. Bill Clinton
   C. Thomas Jefferson
   D. George Washington

4. What is the date of Independence Day?
   A. June 4th
   B. December 25th
   C. July 1st
   D. July 4th

5. What is the 4th of July?
   A. Memorial Day
   B. Valentine's Day
   C. Veteran's Day
   D. Independence Day

Escribe en los espacios vacios

1. The Declaration of Independence was adopted on _____, 1776.
   July 4   December 25

2. The basic belief of the Declaration of Independence is _____.
   America comes first   all men are created equal

3. _____ Day is on the 4th of July.
   Independence   Memorial

4. The main writer of the Declaration of Independence was _____.
   George Washington   Thomas Jefferson

5. Independence Day is on July _____.
   10th   4th

Preguntas de Si o No

Encierra **Si** en un círculo si la oración es correcta. Encierra **No** si la oración no es correcta.

Si   No   The 4th of July is Independence Day.

Si   No   The basic belief of the Declaration of Independence is that all men are created equal.

Si   No   The Declaration of Independence was adopted in 1776.

Si   No   The main writer of the Declaration of Independence was George Washington.

Si   No   The basic belief of the Declaration of Independence is that the people should work seven days a week.

Si   No   The Declaration of Independence was written in 1787.

Si   No   The basic belief of the Declaration of Independence is that the President should have absolute power.

Si   No   The Declaration of Independence was adopted on July 4, 1776.

Si   No   The main writer of the Declaration of Independence was Thomas Jefferson.

Si   No   Independence Day is on December 25th.

PRACTICA DE DICTADO

Escribe cada oración dos veces. La primera vez, copia la lección. La segunda vez, haz que alguien lea la oración mientras la escribes.

1. The woman eats.

2. The woman eats food.

3. The woman eats two apples.

1. _____.

1. _____.

2. _____.

2. _____.

3. _____.

3. _____.

PRACTICA PARA LA ENTREVISTA

Di, repite, en voz alta y muchas veces estas preguntas y respuestas.

Pregunta:	Have you ever claimed in writing or in any other way to be a U.S. citizen?
Respuesta:	No, I have never lied about my status.
Pregunta:	Have you ever claimed in writing or in any other way to be a U.S. citizen?
Respuesta:	No, I never said I was a U.S. citizen.
Pregunta:	Have you ever pretended to be a U.S. citizen?
Respuesta:	No, I have never lied about my citizenship.
Pregunta:	Have you ever claimed in writing to be a U.S. citizen?
Respuesta:	No, I have never pretended to be an American citizen.
Pregunta:	Have you ever claimed in writing or in any other way to be a U.S. citizen?
Respuesta:	No, I am not a U.S. citizen.
Pregunta:	Have you ever voted or registered to vote in the United States?
Respuesta:	No, I have never tried to vote because I am not a U.S. citizen.
Pregunta:	Have you ever voted or registered to vote in the United States?
Respuesta:	No, I am not a U.S. citizen.
Pregunta:	Have you ever voted or registered to vote in the United States?
Respuesta:	No, I have never tried to vote in America.

Tu Turno

Haz que alguien te haga las preguntas anteriores. Responde con las preguntas que sean para tí correctas.

RESPUESTAS DE LA LECCIÓN 15

Preguntas de elección múltiple
1. A. 1776
2. B. all men are created equal
3. C. Thomas Jefferson
4. D. July 4th
5. D. Independence Day

Escribe en los espacios vacios
1. The Declaration of Independence was adopted on <u>July 4</u>, 1776.
2. The basic belief of the Declaration of Independence is <u>all men are created equal</u>.
3. <u>Independence</u> Day is on the 4th of July.
4. The main writer of the Declaration of Independence was <u>Thomas Jefferson</u>.
5. Independence Day is on July <u>4th</u>.

Preguntas de Si o No

(Si)   No   The 4th of July is Independence Day.

(Si)   No   The basic belief of the Declaration of Independence is that all men are created equal.

(Si)   No   The Declaration of Independence was adopted in 1776.

Si   (No)   The main writer of the Declaration of Independence was George Washington.

Si   (No)   The basic belief of the Declaration of Independence is that the people should work seven days a week.

Si   (No)   The Declaration of Independence was written in 1787.

Si   (No)   The basic belief of the Declaration of Independence is that the President should have absolute power.

(Si)   No   The Declaration of Independence was adopted on July 4, 1776.

(Si)   No   The main writer of the Declaration of Independence was Thomas Jefferson.

Si   (No)   Independence Day is on December 25th.

PRUEBA DE REPASO 5

Marca las respuestas para cada pregunta en la hoja que sigue. Las respuestas de esta prueba se pueden encontrar en la última página de la prueba de repaso.

1. (A) (B) (C) (D)   6. (A) (B) (C) (D)
2. (A) (B) (C) (D)   7. (A) (B) (C) (D)
3. (A) (B) (C) (D)   8. (A) (B) (C) (D)
4. (A) (B) (C) (D)   9. (A) (B) (C) (D)
5. (A) (B) (C) (D)

1. Why did the Pilgrims come to America?
   A. to pay taxes
   B. religious freedom
   C. farm land
   D. to escape war

2. What ship brought the Pilgrims to America?
   A. *Maine*
   B. *Nina*
   C. *Mayflower*
   D. *Pinta*

3. What holiday was first celebrated by the American colonists?
   A. Christmas
   B. Halloween
   C. New Year's
   D. Thanksgiving

4. Who helped the Pilgrims in America?
   A. Native Americans
   B. colonists
   C. slaves
   D. President

5. Who was the main writer of the Declaration of Independence?
   A. George Washington
   B. Bill Clinton
   C. Abraham Lincoln
   D. Thomas Jefferson

6. When was the Declaration of Independence written?
   A. July 4, 1778
   B. July 4, 1776
   C. July 4, 1777
   D. July 4, 1771

7. What is the basic belief of the Declaration of Independence?
   A. the President has absolute power
   B. only citizens can vote
   C. all men are created equal
   D. only citizens can live in the United States

8. What were the thirteen original states called?
   A. colonies
   B. territories
   C. provinces
   D. settlements

9. Which one was a colony?
   A. California
   B. Washington
   C. Minnesota
   D. New York

RESPUESTAS DE LA LECCIÓN PRUEBA DE REPASO 5

1. B. religious freedom
2. C. *Mayflower*
3. D. Thanksgiving
4. A. Native Americans
5. D. Thomas Jefferson
6. B. July 4, 1776
7. C. all men are created equal
8. A. colonies
9. D. New York

LECCIÓN 16

La Guerra de Revolución y George Washington

PALABRAS CLAVES

independencia:	libertad
libertad:	emancipación
juramento de fidelidad:	jurar oficialmente ayudar a los Estados Unidos
la Guerra de Revolución:	Guerra entre las trece colonias e Inglaterra

SOBRE LA GUERRA DE REVOLUCION Y GEORGE WASHINGTON

Durante la **Guerra de Revolución,** los Estados Unidos entabló batalla con Inglaterra para poder ganar su **independencia.** Patrick Henry dijo, "Dénme la **libertad** o dénme la muerte." Los colonizadores fueron dirigidos por el primer comandante y jefe de la armada estadounidense, George Washington. Los Estados Unidos ganó su **independencia** de Inglaterra. Después de la **Guerra de Revolución,** George Washington fue elegido por la gente de los Estados Unidos, como primer Presidente. El es conocido como el "padre de nuestro país."

La Guerra Revolucionaria
- Los Estados Unidos peleó con Inglaterra para ganar su independencia
- Los colonizadores fueron dirigidos por George Washington
- George Washington llegó a ser presidente después de la guerra

Turn page for English translation

LESSON 16

Revolutionary War and George Washington

WORDS TO KNOW

independence:	freedom
liberty:	freedom
Oath of Allegiance:	officially swear to help the United States
Revolutionary War:	war between the thirteen colonies and England

ABOUT THE REVOLUTIONARY WAR AND GEORGE WASHINGTON

During the **Revolutionary War**, the United States fought England to gain **independence**. Patrick Henry said, "Give me **liberty** or give me death." The colonists were led by the first commander in chief of the U.S. military, George Washington. The United States gained **independence** from England. After the **Revolutionary War**, George Washington was the first President elected by the people in the United States. He is called the "father of our country."

Revolutionary War
- U.S. fought England to gain independence
- Colonists led by George Washington
- George Washington became president after the war

REPETICIÓN

Di, repite, en voz alta y muchas veces estas preguntas y respuestas.

1. Which President was the first commander in chief of the U.S. military?
   George Washington

2. Who did the United States gain independence from?
   England

3. What country did we fight during the Revolutionary War?
   England

4. Who was the first President elected by the people in the United States?
   George Washington

5. Who said, "Give me liberty or give me death"?
   Patrick Henry

6. Which President is called the "father of our country"?
   George Washington

EJERCICIOS

Los siguientes ejercicios han sido diseñados para familiarizarte con el material de esta lección. El verdadero examen de ciudadanía puede ser oral o un examen de respuestas múltiples.

Preguntas de elección múltiple

Marca tus preguntas a estas preguntas en la hoja que sigue. Las respuestas a todos los ejercicios pueden ser encontradas en la última página de esta lección.

1.	Ⓐ	Ⓑ	Ⓒ	Ⓓ	4.	Ⓐ	Ⓑ	Ⓒ	Ⓓ
2.	Ⓐ	Ⓑ	Ⓒ	Ⓓ	5.	Ⓐ	Ⓑ	Ⓒ	Ⓓ
3.	Ⓐ	Ⓑ	Ⓒ	Ⓓ	6.	Ⓐ	Ⓑ	Ⓒ	Ⓓ

1. Who did the United States gain independence from?
   A. England
   B. France
   C. Spain
   D. Mexico

2. Who is called the "father of our country"?
A. Abraham Lincoln
B. George Washington
C. Bill Clinton
D. Thomas Jefferson

3. Which President was the first commander in chief of the U.S. military?
A. Bill Clinton
B. Abraham Lincoln
C. George Washington
D. Thomas Jefferson

4. Who said, "Give me liberty or give me death"?
A. George Washington
B. Patrick Henry
C. Thomas Jefferson
D. Abraham Lincoln

5. Who was the first President elected by the people in the United States?
A. George Washington
B. Abraham Lincoln
C. Thomas Jefferson
D. John Adams

6. What country did we fight during the Revolutionary War?
A. Spain
B. France
C. England
D. Russia

Escribe en los espacios vacios

1. _____ was the first commander in chief of the U.S. military.
George Washington   Thomas Jefferson

2. Patrick _____ said, "Give me liberty or give me death."
Washington   Henry

3. The U.S. gained independence from _____.
England   France

4. The United States fought _____ during the Revolutionary War.
England   France

5. _____ was the first President elected by the people in the United States.
George Washington   Thomas Jefferson

6. George Washington is called the "father of our _____."
country   state

Preguntas de Si o No

Encierra **Si** en un círculo si la oración es correcta. Encierra **No** si la oración no es correcta.

Si   No   George Washington was the first commander in chief of the U.S. military.

Si   No   America fought France during the Revolutionary War.

Si   No   Thomas Jefferson said, "Give me liberty or give me death."

Si   No   The U.S. gained independence from England.

Si   No   George Washington is called the "father of our country."

Si   No   Patrick Henry said, "Give me life or freedom."

Si   No   America fought England during the Revolutionary War.

Si   No   Patrick Henry said, "Give me liberty or give me death."

Si   No   George Washington was the first President elected by the people in the United States.

PRACTICA DE DICTADO

Escribe cada oración dos veces. La primera vez, copia la lección. La segunda vez, haz que alguien lea la oración mientras la escribes.

1. I have a cat.

2. I have a small cat.

3. I like cats.

1. _____.

1. _____.

2. _____.

2. _____.

3. _____.

3. _____.

PRACTICA PARA LA ENTREVISTA

Di, repite, en voz alta y muchas veces estas preguntas y respuestas.

Pregunta:	Do you believe in the Constitution and the government of the United States?
Respuesta:	Yes, I think the Constitution is a good law.
Pregunta:	Do you believe in the Constitution of the United States?
Respuesta:	Yes, I want to follow the Constitution.
Pregunta:	Do you believe in the government of the United States?
Respuesta:	Yes, I think the government is very good.
Pregunta:	Do you believe in the Constitution and the government of the United States?
Respuesta:	Yes, I believe that the Constitution is a good law.
Pregunta:	Are you willing to take the full Oath of Allegiance to the United States?
Respuesta:	Yes, I am ready to help my new country.
Pregunta:	Are you willing to take the full Oath of Allegiance to the United States?
Respuesta:	Yes, I promise to help my new country. I can't help my old country.
Pregunta:	Are you willing to take the full Oath of Allegiance to the United States?
Respuesta:	Yes, I want to do what is best for America.
Pregunta:	Are you willing to take the full Oath of Allegiance to the United States?
Respuesta:	Yes, I want to officially swear to help the United States.

Tu Turno
Haz que alguien te haga las preguntas anteriores. Responde con las preguntas que sean para tí correctas.

RESPUESTAS DE LA LECCIÓN 16

Preguntas de elección múltiple
1. A. England
2. B. George Washington
3. C. George Washington
4. B. Patrick Henry
5. A. George Washington
6. C. England

Escribe en los espacios vacíos
1. <u>George Washington</u> was the first commander in chief of the U.S. military.
2. Patrick <u>Henry</u> said, "Give me liberty or give me death."
3. The U.S. gained independence from <u>England</u>.
4. The United States fought <u>England</u> during the Revolutionary War.
5. <u>George Washington</u> was the first President elected by the people in the United States.
6. George Washington is called the "father of our <u>country</u>."

Preguntas de Si o No

(Si)   No   George Washington was the first commander in chief of the U.S. military.

Si   **(No)**   America fought France during the Revolutionary War.

Si   **(No)**   Thomas Jefferson said, "Give me liberty or give me death."

(Si)   No   The U.S. gained independence from England.

(Si)   No   George Washington is called the "father of our country."

Si   **(No)**   Patrick Henry said, "Give me life or freedom."

(Si)   No   America fought England during the Revolutionary War.

(Si)   No   Patrick Henry said, "Give me liberty or give me death."

(Si)   No   George Washington was the first President elected by the people in the United States.

LECCIÓN 17

La Guerra Civil

PALABRAS CLAVES

La Guerra Civil:	Guerra entre el Norte y el Sur
incompetente:	que la mente no funciona (loco)
manicomio:	hospital para la gente con problemas mentales
nobleza:	familia que está relacionada con el rey o reina
persecución:	herir a alguien debido a su raza, religión, origen, u opinión política.
esclavo:	alguien que es propiedad de otra persona

SOBRE LA GUERRA CIVIL

De 1861 a 1865, hubo una guerra entre los estados del Norte y los del Sur. Se la conoce como la **Guerra Civil** porque fue peleada entre estados en el mismo país. Muchos estados en el Sur querían formar su propia nación. No querían ser parte de Los Estados Unidos. El Norte quería que todos los estados se mantengan unidos pero sin esclavitud. Una razón para la **Guerra Civil** era la esclavitud. Mucha gente del Sur era dueña de **esclavos**. Mucha gente en el Norte estaba en contra de la esclavitud. El Norte ganó la Guerra.

La Guerra Civil
- El Norte se oponía a la esclavitud
- El Sur apoyaba la esclavitud
- El Sur quería conformar su propia nación
- Tanto el Norte como el Sur pelearon por la esclavitud cosa que dividió al país en dos.
- La Guerra duró de 1861–1865
- El Norte ganó la Guerra

LESSON 17

Civil War

WORDS TO KNOW

Civil War:	war between the North and South
incompetent:	mind does not work (crazy)
mental institution:	hospital for people whose minds don't work
nobility:	family is king or queen or is related to them
persecution:	hurt someone because of their race, religion, national origin, or political opinion
slave:	someone who is owned by another person

ABOUT THE CIVIL WAR

From 1861 to 1865, there was a war between states in the North and states in the South. It was called the **Civil War** because it was fought between states in the same country. Several states in the South wanted to start their own country. They didn't want to be a part of the United States. The North wanted all the states to stay together but without slavery. One reason for the **Civil War** was slavery. Many people in the South owned **slaves**. Many people in the North were against slavery. The North won the war.

The Civil War
- North opposed slavery
- South supported slavery
- South wanted to be their own country
- North and South fought over slavery and breaking the country apart
- War lasted from 1861–1865
- North won the war

REPETICIÓN

Di, repite, en voz alta y muchas veces estas preguntas y respuestas.

1. What was one of the reasons for the Civil War?
   slavery

2. Who wanted to start their own country?
   the South

3. Who wanted the states to stay together?
   the North

4. Who fought during the Civil War?
   the North and South

5. Who won the Civil War?
   the North

EJERCICIOS

Los siguientes ejercicios han sido diseñados para familiarizarte con el material de esta lección. El verdadero examen de ciudadanía puede ser oral o un examen de respuestas múltiples.

Preguntas de elección múltiple

Marca tus preguntas a estas preguntas en la hoja que sigue. Las respuestas a todos los ejercicios pueden ser encontradas en la última página de esta lección.

1. (A) (B) (C) (D)   4. (A) (B) (C) (D)
2. (A) (B) (C) (D)   5. (A) (B) (C) (D)
3. (A) (B) (C) (D)

1. Who wanted the states to stay together?
   A. the South
   B. the North
   C. the West
   D. the East

2. One reason for the Civil War was
   A. freedom of the seas
   B. taxes
   C. slavery
   D. bad leaders

3. Who fought during the Civil War?
   A. East and West
   B. West and East
   C. West and North
   D. North and South

4. Who wanted to start their own country?
   A. the South
   B. the North
   C. the West
   D. the East

5. Who won the Civil War?
   A. the South
   B. the North
   C. the East
   D. the West

Escribe en los espacios vacios

1. _____ wanted to start their own country.
   The North   The South

2. During the Civil War the _____ fought.
   North/South   East/West

3. _____ was one reason for the Civil War.
   Slavery   Taxes

4. The North wanted the states to stay _____.
   together   apart

5. The _____ won the Civil War.
   South   North

Preguntas de Si o No

Encierra **Si** en un círculo si la oración es correcta. Encierra **No** si la oración no es correcta.

Si	No	The East and West fought during the Civil War.
Si	No	The South wanted to start their own country.
Si	No	The South won the Civil War.
Si	No	The North wanted the states to stay together.
Si	No	The North and South fought during the Civil War.
Si	No	One reason for the Civil War was slavery.
Si	No	The North won the Civil War.

PRACTICA DE DICTADO

Escribe cada oración dos veces. La primera vez, copia la lección. La segunda vez, haz que alguien lea la oración mientras la escribes.

1. I wear a hat.

2. I wear a yellow hat.

3. I wear hats.

1. _____.

1. _____.

2. _____.

2. _____.

3. _____.

3. _____.

PRACTICA PARA LA ENTREVISTA

Di, repite, en voz alta y muchas veces estas preguntas y respuestas.

Pregunta: Have you ever been declared legally incompetent or confined as a patient in a mental institution?

Respuesta: No, I am not crazy.

Pregunta: Were you ever in a mental hospital?

Respuesta: No, I am mentally competent.

Pregunta: Have you ever been confined as a patient in a mental institution?

Respuesta: No, I've never been in a mental hospital.

Pregunta: Were you born with or have you acquired any title of nobility?

Respuesta: No, my parents were teachers.

Pregunta: Are you a king, queen, duke, earl, prince, or do you have any other title of nobility?

Respuesta: No, I don't have any special titles along with my name and I am not a king or any other noble.

Pregunta: Were you born with or have you acquired any title of nobility?

Respuesta: No, no one in my family is related to a king or queen.

Pregunta: Have you at any time ever ordered, incited, assisted, or otherwise participated in the persecution of any person because of race, religion, national origin, or political opinion?

Respuesta: No, I have never hurt anyone.

Pregunta: Have you at any time ever ordered or otherwise participated in the persecution of any person because of race, religion, national origin, or political opinion?

Respuesta: No, I don't hurt people because of what they believe or what color they are.

Pregunta: Have you ever participated in the persecution of any person because of race, religion, national origin, or political opinion?

Respuesta: No, I have never persecuted anyone.

Tu Turno

Haz que alguien te haga las preguntas anteriores. Responde con las preguntas que sean para tí correctas.

RESPUESTAS DE LA LECCIÓN 17

Preguntas de elección múltiple
1. B. the North
2. C. slavery
3. D. North and South
4. A. the South
5. B. the North

Escribe en los espacios vacios
1. <u>The South</u> wanted to start their own country.
2. During the Civil War the <u>North/South</u> fought.
3. <u>Slavery</u> was one reason for the Civil War.
4. The North wanted the states to stay <u>together</u>.
5. The <u>North</u> won the Civil War.

Preguntas de Si o No

Si (No)   The East and West fought during the Civil War.

(Si) No   The South wanted to start their own country.

Si (No)   The South won the Civil War.

(Si) No   The North wanted the states to stay together.

(Si) No   The North and South fought during the Civil War.

(Si) No   One reason for the Civil War was slavery.

(Si) No   The North won the Civil War.

LECCIÓN 18

Abraham Lincoln

PALABRAS CLAVES

Proclamación de Emancipación: documento declaratorio de libertad

importancia nacional: de ayuda para los Estados Unidos

servicio de no-combatiente: ayudar a la milicia pero combatir

unido: mantenerse juntos como uno solo

SOBRE ABRAHAM LINCOLN

Durante la Guerra Civil, Abraham Lincoln fue presidente. El quería que el país esté **unido,** y él estaba en contra de la esclavitud. El presidente Lincoln liberó a los esclavos con un escrito llamado **Proclamación de Emancipación.** Después de la Guerra, la **Proclamación de Emancipación** llegó a ser la enmienda numero 13 de la Constitución.

Abraham Lincoln
- Presidente durante la Guerra civil
- En contra de la esclavitud
- Escribió la Proclamación de Emancipación para terminar con la esclavitud

Turn page for English translation

LESSON 18

Abraham Lincoln

WORDS TO KNOW

Emancipation Proclamation: written statement of freedom

national importance: helpful to the United States

noncombatant service: help the military but not fight

united: stay together as one

ABOUT ABRAHAM LINCOLN

Abraham Lincoln was President during the Civil War. He wanted the country to be **united**, and he was against slavery. President Lincoln freed the slaves by writing the **Emancipation Proclamation**. After the war, the **Emancipation Proclamation** became the 13th amendment to the Constitution.

Abraham Lincoln
- President during Civil War
- Against slavery
- Wrote the Emancipation Proclamation to end slavery

REPETICIÓN

Di, repite, en voz alta y muchas veces estas preguntas y respuestas.

1. Who was the President during the Civil War?
Abraham Lincoln

2. What did the Emancipation Proclamation do?
freed many slaves

3. Which President freed the slaves?
Abraham Lincoln

4. What freed the slaves?
Emancipation Proclamation

EJERCICIOS

Los siguientes ejercicios han sido diseñados para familiarizarte con el material de esta lección. El verdadero examen de ciudadanía puede ser oral o un examen de respuestas múltiples.

Preguntas de elección múltiple

Marca tus preguntas a estas preguntas en la hoja que sigue. Las respuestas a todos los ejercicios pueden ser encontradas en la última página de esta lección.

1. Ⓐ Ⓑ Ⓒ Ⓓ   **3.** Ⓐ Ⓑ Ⓒ Ⓓ

2. Ⓐ Ⓑ Ⓒ Ⓓ   **4.** Ⓐ Ⓑ Ⓒ Ⓓ

1. Who freed the slaves?
A. President Lincoln
B. Senator Brown
C. President Jefferson
D. President Washington

2. Who was President during the Civil War?
A. Abraham Lincoln
B. George Washington
C. Bill Clinton
D. Thomas Jefferson

3. What did the Emancipation Proclamation do?
   A. freed the slaves
   B. freed the women
   C. purchased land
   D. expanded the country

4. The slaves were freed by
   A. the Bill of Rights
   B. the Emancipation Proclamation
   C. the Constitution
   D. the Declaration of Independence

Escribe en los espacios vacios

1. President _____ freed the slaves.
   Washington   Lincoln

2. Abraham _____ was President during the Civil War.
   Jefferson   Lincoln

3. The Emancipation Proclamation freed the _____.
   slaves   colonists

4. The _____ won the Civil War.
   South   North

Preguntas de Si o No

Encierra **Si** en un círculo si la oración es correcta. Encierra **No** si la oración no es correcta.

Si   No   George Washington was President during the Civil War.

Si   No   President Lincoln freed the slaves.

Si   No   The Emancipation Proclamation freed the slaves.

Si   No   Abraham Lincoln was President during the Civil War.

Si   No   The slaves were freed by the Emancipation Proclamation.

Si   No   The North won the Civil War.

PRACTICA DE DICTADO

Escribe cada oración dos veces. La primera vez, copia la lección. La segunda vez, haz que alguien lea la oración mientras la escribes.

1. I am learning English.

2. They are learning English.

3. My sisters are learning English.

1. _____.

1. _____.

2. _____.

2. _____.

3. _____.

3. _____.

PRACTICA PARA LA ENTREVISTA

Di, repite, en voz alta y muchas veces estas preguntas y respuestas.

Pregunta: If the law requires it, are you willing to perform noncombatant services in the Armed Forces of the United States?

Respuesta: Yes, I will help the soldiers when the law tells me.

Pregunta: If required by law, are you willing to perform noncombatant services in the Armed Forces of the United States?

Respuesta: Yes, I will do whatever I can to help the military.

Pregunta: Are you willing to perform noncombatant services in the Armed Forces of the United States, if the law says you must?

Respuesta: Yes, I will help the Armed Forces if the law tells me.

Pregunta: If the law requires it, are you willing to perform work of national importance under civilian direction?

Respuesta: Yes, I will do anything to help the United States when the law says I must.

Pregunta:	Are you willing to perform work of national importance under civilian direction, if required by the law?
Respuesta:	Yes, if the law tells me, I will work to help the United States.
Pregunta:	Will you perform work of national importance under civilian direction, when the law says you must?
Respuesta:	Yes, I will do anything to help the United States whenever it is needed.

Tu Turno

Haz que alguien te haga las preguntas anteriores. Responde con las preguntas que sean para tí correctas.

RESPUESTAS DE LA LECCIÓN 18

Preguntas de elección múltiple
1. A. President Lincoln
2. A. Abraham Lincoln
3. A. freed the slaves
4. B. the Emancipation Proclamation

Escribe en los espacios vacíos
1. President <u>Lincoln</u> freed the slaves.
2. Abraham <u>Lincoln</u> was President during the Civil War.
3. The Emancipation Proclamation freed the <u>slaves</u>.
4. The <u>North</u> won the Civil War.

Preguntas de Si o No

Si	(No)	George Washington was President during the Civil War.
(Si)	No	President Lincoln freed the slaves.
(Si)	No	The Emancipation Proclamation freed the slaves.
(Si)	No	Abraham Lincoln was President during the Civil War.
(Si)	No	The slaves were freed by the Emancipation Proclamation.
(Si)	No	The North won the Civil War.

LECCIÓN 19

Historia Después de la Guerra Civil

PALABRAS CLAVES

aliados: amigos en tiempos de Guerra

líder de los derechos civiles: persona que ayuda a otros a creer en la justicia para todas las razas.

reclutado: preguntado para ser soldado

enemigos: la gente contra la cual se pelea

ALGUNOS EVENTOS DE LA HISTORIA DESPUES DE LA GUERRA

Otra Guerra estaba teniendo lugar en los años cuarenta, la llamada Segunda Guerra Mundial. Los **enemigos** de la Segunda Guerra Mundial eran Alemania, Italia, y Japón. Los aliados de los Estados Unidos durante la Segunda Guerra Mundial eran Inglaterra, Francia, China, La Unión Soviética, Canadá, Australia, y Nueva Zelandia. Después de la Segunda Guerra Mundial, se crearon las Naciones Unidas. En las Naciones Unidas, muchos países discuten los problemas del mundo y tratan de resolverlos de una manera pacífica. En los años cincuenta, Alaska fue el estado 49 en unirse a la Unión, y Hawai fue el 50 en hacer lo propio. Estos fueron los últimos dos estados que se unieron a la Unión. Durante los años sesenta, Dr. Martin Luther King, Jr. trabajó como **líder de los derechos civiles**. El trabajó por la igualdad de los derechos de la gente negra y de otros. El encabezó muchas demostraciones pacíficas.

LESSON 19

History after the Civil War

WORDS TO KNOW

allies: friends during war time

civil rights leader: person who helps others believe in justice for all races of
                             people

drafted: asked to be a soldier

enemies: people we fought against

SOME EVENTS IN LATER HISTORY

Another war was going on in the 1940s, called World War II. The United States's **enemies** in World War II were Germany, Italy, and Japan. The United States's **allies** during World War II were England, France, China, the Soviet Union, Canada, Australia, and New Zealand. After World War II, the United Nations was created. At the United Nations, many countries talk about world problems and try to solve them in a peaceful way. In the 1950s, Alaska was the 49th state to join the union and Hawaii was the 50th state to join the union. They were the last two states to join the union. During the 1960s, Dr. Martin Luther King, Jr. worked as a **civil rights leader**. He worked for equal rights for black people and others. He led many peaceful demonstrations.

REPETICIÓN

Di, repite, en voz alta y muchas veces estas preguntas y respuestas.

1. Who were the United States's enemies in World War II?
Germany, Italy, and Japan

2. Who were the United States's allies during World War II?
Britain, Canada, Australia, New Zealand, Russia, China, and France

3. Name one purpose of the United Nations.
for countries to talk about world problems and try to solve them

4. What was the 49th state to join the union?
Alaska

5. What was the 50th state to join the union?
Hawaii

6. Who was Martin Luther King, Jr.?
a civil rights leader

EJERCICIOS

Los siguientes ejercicios han sido diseñados para familiarizarte con el material de esta lección. El verdadero examen de ciudadanía puede ser oral o un examen de respuestas múltiples.

Preguntas de elección múltiple
Marca tus preguntas a estas preguntas en la hoja que sigue. Las respuestas a todos los ejercicios pueden ser encontradas en la última página de esta lección.

1. Ⓐ Ⓑ Ⓒ Ⓓ   **4.** Ⓐ Ⓑ Ⓒ Ⓓ
2. Ⓐ Ⓑ Ⓒ Ⓓ   **5.** Ⓐ Ⓑ Ⓒ Ⓓ
3. Ⓐ Ⓑ Ⓒ Ⓓ   **6.** Ⓐ Ⓑ Ⓒ Ⓓ
7. Ⓐ Ⓑ Ⓒ Ⓓ

1. What is one purpose of the United Nations?
A. to raise taxes
B. for countries to talk about world problems and try to solve them
C. to declare wars
D. to make and enforce laws

2. What was the 49th state to join the union?
  A. Minnesota
  B. New York
  C. Texas
  D. Alaska

3. Who were the United States's enemies in World War II?
  A. Germany, Italy, and Japan
  B. Canada, Russia, and Poland
  C. Mexico and Brazil
  D. Britain and France

4. What was the 50th state to join the union?
  A. New Jersey
  B. Rhode Island
  C. Hawaii
  D. Wisconsin

5. Who was Martin Luther King, Jr.?
  A. civil rights leader
  B. President
  C. senator
  D. tax collector

6. Who were the United States's allies during World War II?
  A. Mexico and Brazil
  B. Chile, Argentina, and Venezuela
  C. Britain, Canada, Australia, New Zealand, Russia, China, and France
  D. Syria, Egypt, Iraq, and Africa

7. The last states to be added to the United States were
  A. Alaska and Hawaii
  B. Puerto Rico and Hawaii
  C. Guam and Hawaii
  D. Alaska and Puerto Rico

Encierra en un círculo la respuesta correcta.

1. Who were two of the United States's enemies in World War II?
  Britain/Canada   Japan/Italy

2. Who were two of the United States's allies in World War II?
  Britain/Canada   Japan/Italy

3. Where do countries talk about world problems and try to solve them?
United Nations   United Justices

4. What was the 49th state to join the union?
Alaska   Connecticut

5. What was the 50th state to join the union?
Utah   Hawaii

6. Who was a civil rights leader?
Martin Luther King   Francis Scott Key

Preguntas de Si o No

Encierra **Si** en un círculo si la oración es correcta. Encierra **No** si la oración no es correcta.

Si   No   Germany and Japan were two of the United States's enemies in World War II.

Si   No   China and Britain were two of the United States's allies in World War II.

Si   No   Countries talk about world problems and try to solve them at the United Nations.

Si   No   Wyoming was the 49th state to join the union.

Si   No   Hawaii was the 50th state to join the union.

Si   No   Martin Luther King, Jr. was a civil rights leader.

Si   No   Russia and France were two of the United States's allies in World War II.

Si   No   Martin Luther King, Jr. was a congressman.

PRACTICA DE DICTADO

Escribe cada oración dos veces. La primera vez, copia la lección. La segunda vez, haz que alguien lea la oración mientras la escribes.

1. I like snow.

2. Today it is snowing.

3. The snow is cold.

1. _____ .

1. _____ .

2. _____ .

2. _____ .

3. _____ .

3. _____ .

PRACTICA PARA LA ENTREVISTA

Dí, repite, en voz alta y muchas veces estas preguntas y respuestas.

Pregunta:	Have you ever left the United States to avoid being drafted into the U.S. Armed Forces?
Respuesta:	No, I have never gone away to avoid going into the military.

Pregunta:	Have you ever left the United States to avoid being drafted?
Respuesta:	No, I have never left the country so I didn't have to go to war.

Pregunta:	Have you ever left the United States so you didn't have to fight in a war?
Respuesta:	No, I have never gone away to avoid being drafted into the military.

Pregunta:	Have you ever failed to comply with Selective Service laws?
Respuesta:	No, I never withheld my name for becoming a soldier.

Pregunta:	Have you ever failed to comply with Selective Service laws?
Respuesta:	No, I have always given my name so I could be called to fight.

Pregunta:	Did you register for the Selective Service?
Respuesta:	Yes, I gave my name to the government.

Pregunta:	Do you know your Selective Service number?
Respuesta:	Yes, I have that number written on this paper.

Tu Turno

Haz que alguien te haga las preguntas anteriores. Responde con las preguntas que sean para tí correctas.

RESPUESTAS DE LA LECCIÓN 19

Preguntas de elección múltiple
1. B. for countries to talk about world problems and try to solve them
2. D. Alaska
3. A. Germany, Italy, and Japan
4. C. Hawaii
5. A. civil rights leader
6. C. Britain, Canada, Australia, New Zealand, Russia, China, and France
7. A. Alaska and Hawaii

Encierra en un círculo la respuesta correcta.
1. Who were two of the United States's enemies in World War II?
   Britain/Canada   (Japan/Italy)
2. Who were two of the United States's allies in World War II?
   (Britain/Canada)   Japan/Italy
3. Where do countries talk about world problems and try to solve them?
   (United Nations)   United Justices
4. What was the 49th state to join the union?
   (Alaska)   Connecticut
5. What was the 50th state to join the union?
   Utah   (Hawaii)
6. Who was a civil rights leader?
   (Martin Luther King Jr.)   Francis Scott Key

Preguntas de Si o No

(Si)   No   Germany and Japan were two of the United States's enemies in World War II.

(Si)   No   China and Britain were two of the United States's allies in World War II.

(Si)   No   Countries talk about world problems and try to solve them at the United Nations.

Si   (No)   Wyoming was the 49th state to join the union.

(Si)   No   Hawaii was the 50th state to join the union.

(Si)   No   Martin Luther King, Jr. was a civil rights leader.

(Sí)   No   Russia and France were two of the United States's allies in World War II.

Sí   (No)   Martin Luther King, Jr. was a congressman.

LECCIÓN 20

Los Estados Unidos de Hoy

PALABRAS CLAVES

alienación: estado de ser un residente nacido en el estranjero

objeciones concientes: rezones por las cuales una persona no pelea en la Guerra

democracia: gobierno de, por, y para la gente

República Democrática: la forma del gobierno de los Estados Unidos

desertado: dejar la milicia sin permiso

exoneración: quedarse fuera

partido político: grupo con ideas de gobierno similares

SOBRE LOS ESTADOS UNIDOS DE HOY

Hoy, en los Estados Unidos, existen cincuenta estados. La capital de los Estados Unidos está en Washington, D.C. Los dos **partidos políticos** más importantes en los Estados Unidos son los demócratas y republicanos. El gobierno de los Estados Unidos es una **República Democratica**, a la cual Abraham Lincoln llamó un "gobierno de la gente, por la gente, y para la gente." Un gobierno donde la gente decide quienes van a ser sus líderes, es llamado una **democracia**.

Los Estados Unidos Hoy
- 50 estados
- 2 partidos políticos (republicano, demócrata)
- República Democrática

LESSON 20

The United States Today

WORDS TO KNOW

alienage:	status of being a foreign-born resident
conscientious objections:	reasons a person will not fight in a war
democracy:	government of, by, and for the people
Democratic Republic:	the form of the U.S. government
deserted:	left the military without permission
exemption:	to stay out of
political party:	group with similar ideas about government

ABOUT THE UNITED STATES TODAY

In the United States today, there are fifty states. The capital of the United States is in Washington, DC. The two major **political parties** in the U.S. are the Democrats and Republicans. The government of the U.S. is a **Democratic Republic**, which Abraham Lincoln called a "government of the people, by the people, and for the people." A government where the people decide who the leaders will be is called a **democracy**.

United States Today
- 50 states
- 2 political parties (Republican, Democrat)
- Democratic Republic

REPETICIÓN

Di, repite, en voz alta y muchas veces estas preguntas y respuestas.

1. How many states are in the United States?
fifty (50)

2. Where is the capital of the U.S.?
Washington, DC

3. What are the two major political parties in the U.S.?
Democrat and Republican

4. What kind of government does the U.S. have?
Democratic Republic

EJERCICIOS

Los siguientes ejercicios han sido diseñados para familiarizarte con el material de esta lección. El verdadero examen de ciudadanía puede ser oral o un examen de respuestas múltiples.

Preguntas de elección múltiple

Marca tus preguntas a estas preguntas en la hoja que sigue. Las respuestas a todos los ejercicios pueden ser encontradas en la última página de esta lección.

1. Ⓐ Ⓑ Ⓒ Ⓓ   **3.** Ⓐ Ⓑ Ⓒ Ⓓ

2. Ⓐ Ⓑ Ⓒ Ⓓ   **4.** Ⓐ Ⓑ Ⓒ Ⓓ

1. Where is the capital of the United States?
A. New York City
B. Washington, DC
C. Philadelphia, PA
D. Los Angeles

2. What kind of government does the U.S. have?
A. Democratic Republic
B. Feudalism
C. Communist
D. Republic of States

3. How many states are in the union?
A. forty-four
B. forty-eight
C. fifty
D. fifty-two

4. What are the two major political parties in the U.S.?
A. Democrat and Republican
B. Communist and Fascist
C. Judicial and Republican
D. Executive and Democratic

Escribe en los espacios vacíos

1. Democrat and Republican are the two major _____ in the United States.
political parties   companies

2. There are _____ states in the United States.
fifty   thirteen

3. _____ and Republican are the two major political parties in the United States.
Congress   Democrat

4. The United States has a Democratic _____ form of government.
States   Republic

5. The capital of the United States is in _____.
New York City   Washington, DC

Preguntas de Si o No

Encierra **Si** en un círculo si la oración es correcta. Encierra **No** si la oración no es correcta.

Si	No	The capital of the United States is in New York City.

Si   No   The capital of the United States is in New York City.

Si   No   The United States has a Democratic Republic form of government.

Si   No   There are fifty states in the U.S.

Si   No   Democrat and Republican are the two major political parties in the United States.

Si   No   The United States has a Communist form of government.

Si   No   The capital of the United States is in Washington, DC.

Si   No   The United States is made up of fifty states.

PRACTICA DE DICTADO

Escribe cada oración dos veces. La primera vez, copia la lección. La segunda vez, haz que alguien lea la oración mientras la escribes.

1. The child plays.

2. The child plays with a toy.

3. The child likes the toy.

1. _____.

1. _____.

2. _____.

2. _____.

3. _____.

3. _____.

PRACTICA PARA LA ENTREVISTA

Di, repite, en voz alta y muchas veces estas preguntas y respuestas.

Pregunta: Did you ever apply for exemption from military service because of alienage, conscientious objections, or other reasons?

Respuesta: No, I have never said that I would not fight for America.

Pregunta: Have you ever tried to avoid military service?

Respuesta: No, I have always been willing to be a soldier.

Pregunta: Did you ever request to stay out of the Armed Forces because of your religious beliefs?

Respuesta: No, my religion says it is okay to protect my country by fighting a war.

Pregunta: Have you ever deserted from the military, air, or naval forces of the United States?

Respuesta: No, I have never even been in the Armed Forces.

Pregunta:	Have you ever deserted from the military, air, or naval forces of the United States?
Respuesta:	No, I was honorably discharged from the army.
Pregunta:	Did you leave the Armed Forces before you were allowed to?
Respuesta:	No, I was in the Armed Forces for a full three years.

Tu Turno

Haz que alguien te haga las preguntas anteriores. Responde con las preguntas que sean para tí correctas.

RESPUESTAS DE LA LECCIÓN 20

Preguntas de elección múltiple

1. B. Washington, DC
2. A. Democratic Republic
3. C. fifty
4. A. Democrat and Republican

Escribe en los espacios vacios

1. Democrat and Republican are the two major <u>political parties</u> in the United States.
2. There are <u>fifty</u> states in America.
3. <u>Democrat</u> and Republican are the two major political parties in the United States.
4. The United States has a Democratic <u>Republic</u> form of government.
5. The capital of the United States is in <u>Washington, DC</u>.

Preguntas de Si o No

Si	(No)	The capital of the United States is in New York City.
(Si)	No	The United States has a Democratic Republic form of government.
(Si)	No	There are fifty states in the U.S.
(Si)	No	Democrat and Republican are the two major political parties in the United States.
Si	(No)	The United States has a Communist form of government.
(Si)	No	The capital of the United States is in Washington, DC.
(Si)	No	The United States is made up of fifty states.

LECCIÓN 21

La Bandera

PALABRAS CLAVES

enseña: bandera

comunista: una persona que pertenece a un partido político que quiere la apropiación común de la producción y distribución de productos.

himno nacional: canción de los Estados Unidos

representar: colocarse por

SOBRE LA BANDERA

Los Estados Unidos tiene una bandera que es de color rojo, blanco, y azul. Hay cincuenta estrellas blancas que **representan** los cincuenta estados de la Unión. Hay trece franjas rojas y blancas que **representan** las trece primeras colonias. Nuestro Himno Nacional es sobre la bandera. El nombre de nuestro **Himno Nacional** es "*The Star-Spangled Banner*," (La **bandera** adornada con estrellas), y fue escrita por Francis Scott Key.

La bandera de los Estados Unidos
- Rojo, blanco, azul
- 50 estrellas (por los 50 estados)
- 13 franjas (por las primeras colonias)

El Himno Nacional
- Se refiere a la bandera de los Estados Unidos
- Escrita por Francis Scott Key

Turn page for English translation

LESSON 21

The Flag

WORDS TO KNOW

banner: flag

Communist: person who belongs to a party that wants common ownership of production and distribution of products

National Anthem: song about America

represent: stand for

ABOUT THE FLAG

The United States has a flag that is red, white, and blue. There are fifty white stars that **represent** the fifty states in the union. There are thirteen red and white stripes that **represent** the original thirteen colonies. Our national anthem is about the flag. The name of our **National Anthem** is "The Star-Spangled **Banner**," and it was written by Francis Scott Key.

The U.S. Flag
- Red, white, blue
- 50 stars (for the 50 states)
- 13 stripes (for the original colonies)

The National Anthem
- Written about the U.S. flag
- Written by Francis Scott Key

REPETICIÓN

Di, repite, en voz alta y muchas veces estas preguntas y respuestas.

1. What are the colors of our flag?
   red, white, blue

2. How many stars are on our flag?
   fifty (50)

3. What color are the stars on our flag?
   white

4. What do the stars on the flag represent?
   The fifty (50) states. There is one star for each state in the union.

5. How many stripes are on the flag?
   thirteen (13)

6. What color are the stripes?
   red and white

7. What do the stripes on the flag represent?
   original thirteen (13) colonies

8. Who wrote "The Star-Spangled Banner"?
   Francis Scott Key

9. What is the national anthem of the United States?
   "The Star-Spangled Banner"

EJERCICIOS

Los siguientes ejercicios han sido diseñados para familiarizarte con el material de esta lección. El verdadero examen de ciudadanía puede ser oral o un examen de respuestas múltiples.

Preguntas de elección múltiple

Marca tus preguntas a estas preguntas en la hoja que sigue. Las respuestas a todos los ejercicios pueden ser encontradas en la última página de esta lección.

1. Ⓐ Ⓑ Ⓒ Ⓓ   6. Ⓐ Ⓑ Ⓒ Ⓓ

2. Ⓐ Ⓑ Ⓒ Ⓓ   7. Ⓐ Ⓑ Ⓒ Ⓓ

3. Ⓐ Ⓑ Ⓒ Ⓓ   8. Ⓐ Ⓑ Ⓒ Ⓓ

4. Ⓐ Ⓑ Ⓒ Ⓓ   9. Ⓐ Ⓑ Ⓒ Ⓓ

5. Ⓐ Ⓑ Ⓒ Ⓓ

1. How many stars are on the flag?
   A. thirteen
   B. forty-four
   C. fifty
   D. fifty-two

2. What are the colors of our flag?
   A. red, white, blue
   B. blue, orange, red
   C. red, white, pink
   D. red, white, green

3. How many stripes are on the flag?
   A. ten
   B. thirteen
   C. fifty
   D. fifty-two

4. What color are the stars on the flag?
   A. red
   B. white
   C. blue
   D. black

5. What do the stripes on the flag represent?
   A. fifty states
   B. original thirteen colonies
   C. Mayflower
   D. pilgrims

6. What do the stars on the flag represent?
A. fifty states
B. original thirteen colonies
C. Mayflower
D. pilgrims

7. What colors are the stripes?
A. red and white
B. blue and white
C. white and blue
D. red and blue

8. What is the national anthem of the United States?
A. The Star-Spangled Banner
B. My Country
C. America the Beautiful
D. Good News America

9. Who wrote "The Star-Spangled Banner"?
A. Abraham Lincoln
B. Senator Brown
C. Francis Scott Key
D. George Washington

Preguntas para agrupar

Responde cada pregunta con la respuesta más apropiada.

____ What do the stripes on the flag represent?	A.	red, white, blue
____ What color are the stripes?	B.	fifty
____ Who wrote "The Star-Spangled Banner"?	C.	white
____ What color are the stars on the flag?	D.	fifty states
____ How many stripes are on the flag?	E.	thirteen
____ What do the stars on the flag represent?	F.	Francis Scott Key
____ What are the colors of our flag?	G.	red and white
____ How many stars are on the flag?	H.	original thirteen colonies
____ What is the national anthem of the United States?	I.	"The Star-Spangled Banner"

Preguntas de Si o No

Encierra **Si** en un círculo si la oración es correcta. Encierra **No** si la oración no es correcta.

Si   No   The stars on the flag are white.

Si   No   The flag is red, white, and blue.

Si   No   The stripes on the flag represent the original thirteen colonies.

Si   No   The flag has twelve stripes on it.

Si   No   Francis Scott Key wrote "The Star-Spangled Banner."

Si   No   The stripes on the flag are red and white.

Si   No   The stars on the flag represent the fifty stars in the sky.

Si   No   The stars on the flag are blue.

Si   No   "The Star-Spangled Banner" is the national anthem of the United States.

Si   No   The flag has fifty stars on it.

PRACTICA DE DICTADO

Escribe cada oración dos veces. La primera vez, copia la lección. La segunda vez, haz que alguien lea la oración mientras la escribes.

1. I can read English.

2. I can write English.

3. I can read, write, and speak English.

1. _____.

1. _____.

2. _____.

2. _____.

3. _____.

3. _____.

PRACTICA PARA LA ENTREVISTA

Di, repite, en voz alta y muchas veces estas preguntas y respuestas.

Pregunta: Are you a member of the Communist Party?
Respuesta: No, I am not a member of any group.

Pregunta: Have you ever been a member of the Communist Party?
Respuesta: No, I never joined that group.

Pregunta: Are you now or have you ever been a member of the Communist Party?
Respuesta: I am not a member now, but I was many years ago.

Pregunta: Why were you a Communist?
Respuesta: I joined because everyone else joined. I didn't believe in it.

Pregunta: When was that?
Respuesta: I joined in 1972, but I never went to the meetings.

Tu Turno

Haz que alguien te haga las preguntas anteriores. Responde con las preguntas que sean para tí correctas.

RESPUESTAS DE LA LECCIÓN 21

Preguntas de elección múltiple

1. C. fifty
2. A. red, white, blue
3. B. thirteen
4. B. white
5. B. original thirteen colonies
6. A. fifty states
7. A. red and white
8. A. The Star-Spangled Banner
9. C. Francis Scott Key

Preguntas para agrupar

_H_ What do the stripes on the flag represent?	A.	red, white, blue
_G_ What color are the stripes?	B.	fifty
_F_ Who wrote "The Star-Spangled Banner"?	C.	white
_C_ What color are the stars on the flag?	D.	fifty states
_E_ How many stripes are on the flag?	E.	thirteen
_D_ What do the stars on the flag represent?	F.	Francis Scott Key
_A_ What are the colors of our flag?	G.	red and white
_B_ How many stars are on the flag?	H.	original thirteen colonies
_I_ What is the national anthem of the United States?	I.	"The Star-Spangled Banner"

Preguntas de Si o No

(Si) No   The stars on the flag are white.

(Si) No   The flag is red, white, and blue.

(Si) No   The stripes on the flag represent the original thirteen colonies.

Si (No)   The flag has twelve stripes on it.

(Si) No   Francis Scott Key wrote "The Star-Spangled Banner."

(Si) No   The stripes on the flag are red and white.

Si (No)   The stars on the flag represent the fifty stars in the sky.

Si (No)   The stars on the flag are blue.

(Si) No   "The Star-Spangled Banner" is the national anthem of the United States.

(Si) No   The flag has fifty stars on it.

LECCIÓN 22

Gobiernos Locales y Estatales

PALABRAS CLAVES

afiliados: concatenados o conectados

capital: ciudad donde el gobierno está ubicado

SOBRE LOS GOBIERNOS LOCALES Y ESTATALES

Cada estado tiene su propia **capital**. Necesitas saber cuál es la **capital** de tu estado. Por ejemplo, la **capital** de Texas es Austin, la **capital** del estado de Nueva York es Albany, y la capital de Florida es Tallahassee. Cada estado tiene un gobernador como la cabeza ejecutiva. Cada estado tiene también dos senadores quienes representan a ese estado en Washington, D.C. Dentro de cada estado hay muchos gobiernos locales. Cada ciudad tiene un alcalde como su cabeza ejecutiva.

Estado
- La Capital es donde se encuentra el gobierno
- El gobernador es la cabeza ejecutiva
- Dos (2) senadores representan cada estado en Washington, DC

LESSON 22

State and Local Governments

WORDS TO KNOW

affiliated: linked or connected

capital: city where the government is located

ABOUT STATE AND LOCAL GOVERNMENTS

Each state has its own **capital**. You need to know what the **capital** of your state is. For example, the **capital** of Texas is Austin, the **capital** of New York state is Albany, and the capital of Florida is Tallahassee. Every state has a governor as its head executive. Each state also has two senators who represent that state in Washington, DC. Within each state are many local governments. Each city has a mayor as its head executive.

State
- Capital is where the government is located
- Governor is the head executive
- Two (2) senators represent each state in Washington, DC

REPETICIÓN

Write in the answers to these questions and then say the questions and answers many times out loud.

1. What is the capital of your state? _____

2. Who is the current governor of your state? _____

3. Who are the two senators from your state? _____

4. Who is the head of your local government? _____

EJERCICIOS

Los siguientes ejercicios han sido diseñados para familiarizarte con el material de esta lección. El verdadero examen de ciudadanía puede ser oral o un examen de respuestas múltiples.

Escribe en los espacios vacios

Pregunta a un profesor, o a un familiar las respuestas a las siguientes preguntas. Si no puedes encontrar la respuesta a una de estas preguntas, anda a la biblioteca pública y pregunta al bibliotecario. Escribe las respuestas que encuentres en los espacios en blanco que siguen.

1. The head of your local government is _____.

2. _____ is the capital of your state.

3. The governor of your state is _____.

4. The two senators from your state are _____ and _____.

5. _____ is the mayor of your city.

Copia los Oraciones

Copia dos veces cada oración que sigue después de que hayas llenado los espacios en blanco.

1. The head of my local government is _____.

_____.

_____.

2. The governor of my state is _____.

_____.

_____.

3. The two senators from my state are _____ and

_____.

_____.

_____.

PRACTICA DE DICTADO

Escribe cada oración dos veces. La primera vez, copia la lección. La segunda vez, haz que alguien lea la oración mientras la escribes.

1. Today is Tuesday.

2. Tomorrow is Wednesday.

3. Today it is windy.

1. _____.

1. _____.

2. _____.

2. _____.

3. _____.

3. _____.

PRACTICA PARA LA ENTREVISTA

Di, repite, en voz alta y muchas veces estas preguntas y respuestas.

Pregunta: Have you ever been affiliated with the Nazi Party?
Respuesta: No, I don't agree with the Nazi Party.

Pregunta: Have you ever been a member of the Nazi Party?
Respuesta: No, I never joined the Nazi Party.

Pregunta:	Did you help the Nazi government in any way?
Respuesta:	No, I never assisted the Nazis.
Pregunta:	Were you a part of the Nazi Party between 1933 and 1945?
Respuesta:	No, I don't agree with the Nazi Party.
Pregunta:	Have you ever helped the Nazi Party?
Respuesta:	No, I don't like the Nazi Party.
Pregunta:	Are you a member of any clubs or organizations?
Respuesta:	No, I am not a part of any organized groups.
Pregunta:	Are you a member of any clubs or organizations?
Respuesta:	Yes, I am a member of the Small Business Association.
Pregunta:	Are you a member of any clubs?
Respuesta:	No, I do not take part in any clubs.

Tu Turno

Haz que alguien te haga las preguntas anteriores. Responde con las preguntas que sean para tí correctas.

LECCIÓN 23

Ciudadanos Americanos

PALABRAS CLAVES

beneficios:	cosas buenas
testimonio falso:	decir una mentira
mínimo:	el número más pequeño

SOBRE LOS CIUDADANOS AMERICANOS

El derecho más importante otorgado a un ciudadano estadounidense (americano), es el derecho de votar. La edad **mínima** para votar en los Estados Unidos es 18 años. La enmiendas a la constitución que garantizan o tratan de los derechos al voto son 15ta, 19na, 24ta, y 26ta. Existen muchos **beneficios** para convertirse en ciudadano americano, como por ejemplo, el derecho al voto, el derecho de viajar con un pasaporte americano, el derecho de servir como jurado, y el derecho de solicitar empleos federales. El formulario del INS que se usa para solicitar convertirse en ciudadano naturalizado es Form N-400 "*Application for Naturalization*" (Solicitud para Naturalización).

Voto
- La edad mínima para votar es 18
- 15ta, 19na, 24ta, y 26ta enmiendas a la Constitución discuten el derecho al voto

Beneficios de la Ciudadanía
- Derecho al voto
- Derecho de viajar con pasaporte americano
- Derecho de servir como jurado
- Derecho de solicitar empleos o trabajos federales

Turn page for English translation

LESSON 23

American Citizens

WORDS TO KNOW

benefits:	good things
false testimony:	tell a lie
minimum:	the lowest number allowed

ABOUT AMERICAN CITIZENS

The most important right granted to U.S. citizens is the right to vote. The **minimum** voting age in the United States is eighteen. The amendments to the Constitution that guarantee or discuss voting rights are the 15th, 19th, 24th, and the 26th. There are many **benefits** to becoming a U.S. citizen, such as the right to vote, the right to travel with a U.S. passport, the right to serve on a jury, and the right to apply for federal jobs. The INS form that is used to apply to become a naturalized citizen is Form N-400 "Application for Naturalization."

Voting
- Minimum voting age is 18
- 15th, 19th, 24th, and the 26th amendments to the Constitution discuss voting

Benefits of Citizenship
- Right to vote
- Right to travel with a U.S. passport
- Right to serve on a jury
- Right to apply for federal jobs

REPETICIÓN

Di, repite, en voz alta y muchas veces estas preguntas y respuestas.

1. What is the most important right granted to U.S. citizens?
   right to vote

2. What is the minimum voting age in the United States?
   eighteen (18)

3. Which amendments to the Constitution guarantee or discuss voting rights?
   15th, 19th, 24th, and 26th

4. What are some of the benefits to becoming a United States citizen?
   right to vote, right to travel with a U.S. passport, right to serve on a jury, right to apply for federal jobs

5. What INS form is used to apply to become a naturalized citizen?
   N-400 "Application for Naturalization"

EJERCICIOS

Los siguientes ejercicios han sido diseñados para familiarizarte con el material de esta lección. El verdadero examen de ciudadanía puede ser oral o un examen de respuestas múltiples.

Preguntas de elección múltiple

Marca tus preguntas a estas preguntas en la hoja que sigue. Las respuestas a todos los ejercicios pueden ser encontradas en la última página de esta lección.

1. (A) (B) (C) (D)   4. (A) (B) (C) (D)
2. (A) (B) (C) (D)   5. (A) (B) (C) (D)
3. (A) (B) (C) (D)

1. Which of the following is a benefit of becoming a U.S. citizen?
   A. right to pay taxes
   B. right to vote
   C. right to go to school
   D. right to work

2. Which amendment to the Constitution guarantees or discusses voting rights?
   A. third
   B. fifth
   C. twelfth
   D. fifteenth

3. What is the minimum voting age in the United States?
   A. sixteen
   B. eighteen
   C. twenty-one
   D. twenty-five

4. What is the most important right granted to U.S. citizens?
   A. right to work
   B. right to pay taxes
   C. right to go to school
   D. right to vote

5. What INS form is used to apply to become a naturalized citizen?
   A. N-200 "Petition for Naturalization"
   B. N-400 "Application for Naturalization"
   C. Social Security Card
   D. Form 2000

Encierra en un círculo la respuesta correcta.

1. Which amendment to the Constitution guarantees or discusses voting rights?
   third   twenty-fourth

2. What is the most important right granted to U.S. citizens?
   right to work   right to vote

3. What is the minimum voting age in the United States?
   sixteen   eighteen

4. What is a benefit of becoming a U.S. citizen?
   right to travel with a U.S. passport   right to own a home

5. What INS form is used to apply to become a naturalized citizen?
   N-400 "Application for Naturalization"   N-200 "Petition for Naturalization"

Preguntas de Si o No

Encierra **Si** en un círculo si la oración es correcta. Encierra **No** si la oración no es correcta.

Si	No	The minimum voting age in the United States is twenty-one.
Si	No	The right to vote is the most important right granted to U.S. citizens.
Si	No	The right to travel with a U.S. passport is granted to U.S. citizens.
Si	No	The 15th, 19th, 24th, and 26th amendments to the Constitution guarantee or discuss voting rights.
Si	No	The right to bear arms is the most important right granted to U.S. citizens.
Si	No	The N-400 "Application for Naturalization" is the INS form you use to apply to become a U.S. citizen.
Si	No	Eighteen is the minimum voting age in the United States.

PRACTICA DE DICTADO

Escribe cada oración dos veces. La primera vez, copia la lección. La segunda vez, haz que alguien lea la oración mientras la escribes.

1. It is cold.

2. It is cold outside.

3. I like cold weather.

1. _____.

1. _____.

2. _____.

2. _____.

3. _____.

3. _____.

PRACTICA PARA LA ENTREVISTA

Di, repite, en voz alta y muchas veces estas preguntas y respuestas.

Pregunta: Have you ever given false testimony to obtain an immigration benefit?

Respuesta: No, I have never lied.

Pregunta: Have you ever lied to obtain an immigration benefit?

Respuesta: No, I have never given false testimony.

Pregunta: Have you ever lied at an immigration interview when you were under oath?

Respuesta: No, I have never lied after swearing to tell the truth.

Pregunta: If the law requires it, are you willing to bear arms on behalf of the United States?

Respuesta: Yes, I will fight in a war to help the United States.

Pregunta: If the law requires it, are you willing to bear arms on behalf of the United States?

Respuesta: Yes, I will be a soldier if the law tells me.

Pregunta: Are you willing to bear arms for the United States, even if it is against the country you used to live in?

Respuesta: Yes, I will fight for the United States even if it is against my old country.

Tu Turno

Haz que alguien te haga las preguntas anteriores. Responde con las preguntas que sean para tí correctas.

RESPUESTAS DE LA LECCIÓN 23

Preguntas de elección múltiple
1. B. right to vote
2. D. fifteenth
3. B. eighteen
4. D. right to vote
5. B. N-400 "Application for Naturalization"

Encierra en un círculo la respuesta correcta.
1. Which amendment to the Constitution guarantees or discusses voting rights?
   third   (twenty-fourth)
2. What is the most important right granted to U.S. citizens?
   right to work   (right to vote)
3. What is the minimum voting age in the United States?
   sixteen   (eighteen)
4. What is a benefit of becoming a U.S. citizen?
   right to own a home   (right to travel with a U.S. passport)
5. What INS form is used to apply to become a naturalized citizen?
   (N-400 "Application for Naturalization")   N-200 "Petition for Naturalization"

Preguntas de Si o No

Si   (No)   The minimum voting age in the United States is twenty-one.

(Si)   No   The right to vote is the most important right granted to U.S. citizens.

(Si)   No   The right to travel with a U.S. passport is granted to U.S. citizens.

(Si)   No   The 15th, 19th, 24th, and 26th amendments to the Constitution guarantee or discuss voting rights.

Si   (No)   The right to bear arms is the most important right granted to U.S. citizens.

(Si)   No   The N-400 "Application for Naturalization" is the INS form you use to apply to become a U.S. citizen.

(Si)   No   Eighteen is the minimum voting age in the United States.

PRUEBA DE REPASO 6

Marca las respuestas para cada pregunta en la hoja que sigue. Las respuestas de esta prueba se pueden encontrar en la última página de la prueba de repaso.

1. Ⓐ Ⓑ Ⓒ Ⓓ   9. Ⓐ Ⓑ Ⓒ Ⓓ
2. Ⓐ Ⓑ Ⓒ Ⓓ   10. Ⓐ Ⓑ Ⓒ Ⓓ
3. Ⓐ Ⓑ Ⓒ Ⓓ   11. Ⓐ Ⓑ Ⓒ Ⓓ
4. Ⓐ Ⓑ Ⓒ Ⓓ   12. Ⓐ Ⓑ Ⓒ Ⓓ
5. Ⓐ Ⓑ Ⓒ Ⓓ   13. Ⓐ Ⓑ Ⓒ Ⓓ
6. Ⓐ Ⓑ Ⓒ Ⓓ   14. Ⓐ Ⓑ Ⓒ Ⓓ
7. Ⓐ Ⓑ Ⓒ Ⓓ   15. Ⓐ Ⓑ Ⓒ Ⓓ
8. Ⓐ Ⓑ Ⓒ Ⓓ

1. How many senators does your state have?
   A. one
   B. two
   C. three
   D. four

2. Which countries were our enemies during World War II?
   A. Mexico, Canada, England
   B. Spain, Italy, France
   C. Russia, France, England
   D. Germany, Italy, Japan

3. Who was Martin Luther King, Jr.?
   A. President
   B. Supreme Court justice
   C. civil rights leader
   D. governor

4. What are the 49th and 50th states of the union?
   A. Iowa and Minnesota
   B. Michigan and Illinois
   C. Washington and Montana
   D. Alaska and Hawaii

5. What is the minimum voting age in the United States?
   A. seventeen
   B. sixteen
   C. twenty-one
   D. eighteen

6. What is the most important right granted to U.S. citizens?
   A. right to vote
   B. right to bear arms
   C. right to travel
   D. right to work

7. How many states are in the union?
   A. thirty
   B. forty
   C. fifty
   D. sixty

8. What are the two main political parties in the U.S.?
   A. Communist and Fascist
   B. Democrat and Republican
   C. Partisan and Democratic
   D. Judicial and Republican

9. What form of government does the U.S. have?
   A. Democratic Republic
   B. Communist
   C. Fascist
   D. Fundamentalist

10. What are the colors of our flag?
    A. red, white, blue
    B. blue, orange, red
    C. red, white, pink
    D. red, white, green

11. How many stripes are on the flag?
   A. ten
   B. thirteen
   C. fifty
   D. fifty-two

12. What do the stripes on the flag represent?
   A. fifty states
   B. original thirteen colonies
   C. Mayflower
   D. pilgrims

13. What do the stars on the flag represent?
   A. fifty states
   B. original thirteen colonies
   C. Mayflower
   D. pilgrims

14. Who were the United States's allies during World War II?
   A. Mexico and Brazil
   B. Chile, Argentina, and Venezuela
   C. Britain, Canada, Australia, New Zealand, Russia, China, and France
   D. Syria, Egypt, Iraq, and Africa

15. What is one purpose of the United Nations?
   A. to raise taxes
   B. for countries to talk about world problems and try to solve them
   C. to declare wars
   D. to make and enforce laws

RESPUESTAS DE LA LECCIÓN PRUEBA DE REPASO 6

1. B. two
2. D. Germany, Italy, Japan
3. C. civil rights leader
4. D. Alaska and Hawaii
5. D. eighteen
6. A. right to vote
7. C. fifty
8. B. Democrat and Republican
9. A. Democratic Republic
10. A. red, white, blue
11. B. thirteen
12. B. original thirteen colonies
13. A. fifty states
14. C. Britain, Canada, Australia, New Zealand, Russia, China, and France
15. B. for countries to talk about world problems and try to solve them

CAPÍTULO 5

Palabras y Términos para Aprender

Esta lista contiene términos y definiciones importantes para la ciudadanía. Estudia la lista para aprender lo que cada palabra significa. Estar familiarizado con estas palabras te ayudará a pasar el examen de ciudanía. La palabra y su definición estan incluidas tanto en inglés como en español.

a

abolish	to destroy completely
eliminar	*destrozar completamente*
address	where you live
dirección	*donde vives*
adopted	put into effect
adoptado	*poner en efecto*
advises	gives help to
aconsejar	*da ayuda a alguien*
affiliated	linked or connected
afiliado	*ligado o conectado*
alienage	status of being a foreign-born resident
extranjería	*estado civil de ser un ciudadano extranjero*

allies	friends during war time
aliados	*amigos durante tiempo de guerra*
amendments	changes
enmiendas	*cambios*
appointed	chosen or selected
nombrado	*elegido o seleccionado*
arrested	formally charged by a police officer
arrestado	*formalmente acusado por un oficial de policía*
asylum	protection and immunity from extradition granted by a government to a political refugee from another country.
asilo	*protección e inmunidad contra la extradición otorgada por un gobierno a un refugiado de otro país*

b

banner	flag
bandera	*bandera*
basic belief	main idea, most important part
creencia fundamental	*idea principal, la parte más importante*
bear arms	carry a gun or weapon
portar armas	*llevar una pistola o un arma*
benefits	good things, advantages
beneficios	*buenas cosas, ventajas*
Bill of Rights	first ten amendments of the Constitution that tell the rights you have
la Declaración de Derechos	*las primeras diez enmiendas a la Constitución que te dice los derechos que tienes*
birth place	country where you were born
lugar de nacimiento	*país donde naciste*
born	when a baby comes into the world
nacer	*cuando un bebé llega al mundo*
branches	separate parts
divisiones	*partes separadas*

Cabinet	fourteen people who help the President make decisions
Gabinete	*catorce personas que ayudan al presidente a hacer decisiones*
capital	city where the government is located
capital	*ciudad donde se encuentra el gobierno*
Capitol	where Congress meets
Capitolio	*donde el Congreso se reúne*
chief justice	head of the Supreme Court
juez principal	*jefe de la Corte Suprema*
citizen	A native, inhabitant, or denizen of a particular place.
ciudadano	*un nativo, habitante o originario de un lugar determinado*
citizenship	the country where you have the right to fully participate in he benefits and laws of that country
ciudadanía	*el país en el cual tienes el derecho de participar totalmente de los beneficios y las leyes de ese país*
civil rights leader	person who helps others believe in justice for all races of people
líder de derechos civiles	*persona que ayuda a otros a creer en la justicia para todas las razas*
Civil War	war between the North and South
la Guerra Civil	*guerra entre el Norte y el Sur*
claimed	said something was true; pretended
pretendido	*decir que algo era cierto; pretendido*
colonies	original thirteen states in America
colonias	*originales trece estados de los Estados Unidos*
Communist	person who belongs to a party that wants common owner-ship of property
Comunista	*persona que pertenece a un partido político y que quiere la pertenencia común de propiedades*
Congress	people who make our laws
el Congreso	*grupo de gente que hace nuestras leyes*

conscientious objections	reasons a person will not fight in a war
objeción de conciencia	*razones por las cuales una persona no peleará en una guerra*
Constitution	supreme law of the United States
la Constitución	*ley suprema de los Estados Unidos*
crime	breaking the law
delito	*rompiendo las leyes*

d

Declaration of Independence	written statement saying the colonies wanted to be free from England
la Declaración de la Independencia	*declaración escrita que estableció que las colonias querían ser independientes de Inglaterra*
democracy	government of, by, and for the people
democracia	*gobierno de, por, y para la gente*
Democratic Republic	the form of the U.S. government
República Democrática	*la forma del gobierno de los Estados Unidos*
deported	a judge in court ordered you to go back to your first country
deportado	*un juez de la corte te ordena que regreses a tu país*
deserted	left the military without permission
desertado	*dejar el ejercito sin ningún permiso*
different	another
distinto	*otro*
drafted	asked to be a soldier
llamado a filas	*reclutado como soldado*

e

Electoral College	group who elects the President
Colegio Electoral	*grupo que elije al presidente*

Emancipation Proclamation	written statement of freedom
la Proclamación de la Emancipación de los esclavos	*declaración de libertad escrita*
employer	the name of the company or person you work for
patrón	*el nombre de la persona o companía para la que trabajas*
enemies	people we fight in a war
enemigos	*gente contra la que uno lucha en tiempo de guerra*
executive branch	the part of the government made up of the President, Vice President, and Cabinet
poder ejecutivo	*la parte del gobierno constituida por el Presidente, Vice Presidente y el Gabinete*
exemption	to stay out of
exención	*estar fuera de lugar, mantenerse fuera*
explain	give detailed information
explicar	*dar información detallada*

f, g, h

false testimony	tell a lie
testimonio falso	*decir una mentira*
governor	leader of a state
gobernador	*líder de un estado*
head executive	the leader or person in charge
director ejecutivo	*el lídero persona a cargo*

i

illegal	against the law
ilegales	*encontra de la ley*
inaugurated	sworn into office
investido	*inaugurado en un puesto*
income tax	if you work in the United States, this is the money you pay to the government
impuesto sobre la renta	*si trabajas en los Estados Unidos, éste es el dinero que debes pagar al gobierno*

incompetent	mind does not work (crazy)
incompetente	*la mente no funciona (loco)*
independence	freedom
independencia	*libertad*
Independence Day	July 4th
el Día de la Independencia	*Julio 4*
interpret	to explain
interpretar	*para explicar*
introduction	the beginning
introducción	*el principio*

j, l

job	work or duty
deber	*trabajo u obligación*
judicial branch	the part of the government that includes the Supreme Court
poder judicial	*parte del gobierno que incluye la Corte Suprema*
legislative branch	Congress
poder legislativo	*Congreso*
liberty	freedom
libertad	*libertad*

m

maiden name	a woman's last name before getting married
apellido de soltera	*apellido paterno de una mujer antes de casarse*
marital status	if you are single, married, or divorced
estado civil	*si eres soltero(a), casado(a), o divorciado(a)*
mayor	leader of a city
alcalde	*alcalde de una ciudad*
mental institution	hospital for people whose minds don't work
manicomio	*hospital para gente con problemas mentales*
minimum	the lowest number allowed
mínimo	*el menor número permitido*

n

national anthem *himno nacional*	song about the United States *canción acerca de los Estados Unidos*
national importance *interés nacional*	helpful to the United States *de ayuda para los Estados Unidos*
Native Americans *Indio Americano*	people who lived in America when the pilgrims arrived *gente que vivía en los Estados Unidos antes de la llegada de los Peregrinos (Pilgrims)*
natural born citizen *ciudadano de nacimiento*	person who is born in a country *una persona que nace en un país*
noncombatant service *servicio de no combate*	help the military but not fight *ayudar a los militares pero no pelear*

o

oath *juramento*	promise to tell the truth *prometer decir la verdad*
Oath of Allegiance *Juramento de Fidelidad*	officially swear to help the United States *jurar oficialmente ayuda a los Estados Unidos*
occupation *ocupación*	the name of your job *el nombre de tu trabajo*

p

passport *pasaporte*	An official government document that certifies one's identity and citizenship and permits a citizen to travel abroad *un documento gubernamental oficial que certifica la identidad y ciudadanía de uno y que permite a un ciudadano viajar al exterior*
persecution *persecución*	hurt someone because of their race, religion, national origin, or political opinion *herir a alguien debido a su raza, religion, origen, u opinión política*

pilgrims
peregrinos

people who came to America on a ship called the Mayflower
gente que vino a los Estados Unidos en un barco llamado "Mayflower"

political party
partido político

group with similar ideas about government
grupo con las mismas ideas sobre el gobierno

port of entry
puerto de entrada

place where you arrived in the country
lugar por el cual uno entra a un determinado país

preamble
preámbulo

the introduction to the Constitution
la introducción a la Constitución

r

re-elected
reelegido

voted into office again
elegido por votación y puesto al mando

registered
inscrito

officially signed up to do something
oficialmente asignado a hacer algo

represent
representar

stand for
representar algo o a alguien

representatives
representantes

people who work in the House of Representatives
gente que trabaja en la Casa de Representantes

Revolutionary War
la Guerra de la Independencia

war between the thirteen colonies and England
guerra entre las trece colonias e Inglaterra

s

Selective Service

registering with the U.S. government in case your services are needed

Servicios Selectivos

registrarse con el gobierno estadounidense en caso de que tus servicios sean requeridos

senators
senadores

people who work in the Senate
gente que trabaja en el Senado

slave
esclavo

someone who is owned by another person
alguien que pertenece a otra persona

smuggle
pasar de contrabando

illegally sneaking someone or something into the country
haciendo pasar ilegalmente en el país a alguien o algo

Supreme Court *el Tribunal Supremo*	highest court in the United States *la corte más alta en los Estados Unidos*
supreme law *Ley Suprema*	the highest, most important law *la ley más alta y más importante*

t

term *período*	how long someone works in government *el periodo de tiempo que una persona trabaja en el gobierno*
tried *juzgado*	put through a trial with a judge and jury *puesto en juicio con un juez y un jurado*

u, w

union *unión*	United States of America *Estados Unidos de America*
united *unido*	stay together as one *permanecer juntos como uno solo*
warrant *orden judicial*	official permission from a judge *permiso official de un juez*
White House *Casa Blanca*	place where President lives while serving as President *pugar donde el presidente vive mientras desempeña su función*

CAPÍTULO 6

Historia Oficial del Servicio de Inmigración y Naturalización

(Immigration and Naturalization Services, INS*),* y Preguntas Cívicas

Esta es una lista, ordenada por categorias, de toda la historia official del INS más las preguntas cívicas y sus respuestas. Necesitas saber las respuestas a muchas de las preguntas. Cubre las respuestas y trata de responder cada pregunta correctamente. Seguidamente ve las respuestas para ver si tienes algún error. Ve las respuestas para ver si están correctas. Todas estas preguntas ya han sido hechas en las veintitrés lecciones anteriores.

LA ESTRUCTURA GUBERNAMENTAL

1. How many branches are there in the government?
2. What are the three branches of our government?

1. three (3)
2. executive, legislative, judicial

LA RAMA LEGISLATIVA

3. What is the legislative branch of our government?

3. Congress

4. Who makes the laws in the United States?	**4.** Congress
5. What is Congress?	**5.** Senate and House of Representatives
6. What are the duties of Congress?	**6.** to make laws
7. Who elects Congress?	**7.** the people
8. Where does Congress meet?	**8.** Capitol in Washington, DC
9. How many senators are there in Congress?	**9.** 100 (one hundred)
10. Why are there 100 senators in Congress?	**10.** two (2) from each state
11. Who are the two senators from your state?	**11.** Pregunta a un profesor, o a un familiar la respuesta a la preguntas.
12. How long do we elect each senator?	**12.** six (6) years
13. How many times can a senator be re-elected?	**13.** no limit
14. How many representatives are there in Congress?	**14.** 435 (four hundred thirty-five)
15. How long do we elect the representatives?	**15.** two (2) years
16. How many times can a representative be re-elected?	**16.** no limit

LA RAMA JUDICIAL

17. What is the judicial branch of our government?	**17.** Supreme Court
18. What are the duties of the Supreme Court?	**18.** to interpret laws
19. Who is the chief justice of the Supreme Court?	**19.** William Rehnquist
20. Who selects the Supreme Court justices?	**20.** President
21. How many Supreme Court justices are there?	**21.** nine (9)
22. What is the highest court in the United States?	**22.** Supreme Court

LA RAMA EJECUTIVA

23. What is the executive branch of our government?	**23.** President, Vice President, Cabinet
24. Who was the first President of the United States?	**24.** George Washington

25. Who is the President of the United States today?

25. George W. Bush

26. Who is the Vice President today?

26. Richard Cheney

27. Who elects the President of the United States?

27. the Electoral College

28. How long do we elect the President?

28. four (4) years

29. Who becomes President of the United States if the President should die?

29. Vice President

30. How many terms can a President serve?

30. two (2)

31. Who becomes President of the United States if the President and Vice President should die?

31. Speaker of the House of Representatives

32. What are the requirements to be President?

32. natural born citizen of the U.S., thirty-five (35) years old, lived in the U.S. fourteen (14) years

33. What special group advises the President?

33. Cabinet

34. What is the White House?

34. President's official home

35. Where is the White House located?

35. Washington, DC

36. In what month do we vote for the President?

36. November

37. In what month is the new President inaugurated?

37. January

38. What is the head executive of a state government called?

38. governor

39. What is the head executive of a city government called?

39. mayor

40. Who signs bills into law?

40. President

41. What is the name of the President's official home?

41. White House

42. Who is commander in chief of the U.S. military?

42. President

43. Who has the power to declare war?

43. Congress

LA CONSTITUCION

44. What is the Constitution?

44. the supreme law of the land

45. Can the Constitution be changed?

45. yes

46. What do we call changes to the Constitution?

46. amendments

47. How many amendments are there?

47. twenty-seven (27)

48. What is the supreme law of the United States?

49. When was the Constitution written?

50. What is the Bill of Rights?

51. Where does freedom of speech come from?

52. Whose rights are guaranteed by the Constitution and the Bill of Rights?

53. What is the introduction to the Constitution called?

54. What are the first ten amendments to the Constitution called?

55. Name three rights or freedoms

56. Name one right guaranteed by the first amendment.

57. What is the most important right granted to U.S. citizens?

48. Constitution

49. 1787

50. the first ten (10) amendments

51. the Bill of Rights

52. everyone in the United States, including non-citizens

53. the preamble

54. the Bill of Rights

55.
1. The freedom of speech, guaranteed by the Bill of Rights. press, and religion
2. Right to bear arms
3. Government may not put soldiers in people's homes
4. Government may not search or take a person's property without a warrant
5. A person may not be tried for the same crime twice
6. A person charged with a crime has rights including the right to a trial and a lawyer
7. People are protected from unreasonable fines or cruel punishment

56. freedom of: speech, press, religion, peaceable assembly, and requesting change of government

57. right to vote

58. What is the minimum voting age in the United States?

58. eighteen (18)

LA HISTORIA DE LOS ESTADOS UNIDOS

59. What is the 4th of July?

59. Independence Day

60. When was the Declaration of Independence adopted?

60. July 4, 1776

61. What is the basic belief of the Declaration of Independence?

61. All men are created equal.

62. Who was the main writer of the Declaration of Independence?

62. Thomas Jefferson

63. What is the date of Independence Day?

63. July 4th

64. Which President was the first commander in chief of the U.S. military?

64. George Washington

65. Who did the United States gain independence from?

65. England

66. What country did we fight during the Revolutionary War?

66. England

67. Who said, "Give me liberty or give me death"?

67. Patrick Henry

68. Which President is called the "father of our country"?

68. George Washington

69. Why did the Pilgrims come to America?

69. religious freedom

70. Who helped the Pilgrims in America?

70. Native Americans

71. What ship brought the Pilgrims to America?

71. Mayflower

72. What holiday was celebrated for first time by the American colonists?

72. Thanksgiving

73. What were the thirteen original states called?

73. colonies

74. Can you name the original thirteen states?

74. Connecticut, Delaware, Georgia, Maryland, Massachusetts, New Hampshire, New Jersey, New York, North Carolina, Pennsylvania, Rhode Island, South Carolina, Virginia

75. Who wrote "The Star-Spangled Banner"?

75. Francis Scott Key

76. What is the national anthem of the United States?

76. "The Star-Spangled Banner"

77. Who was the President during the Civil War?	77. Abraham Lincoln
78. What did the Emancipation Proclamation do?	78. freed many slaves
79. Which President freed the slaves?	79. Abraham Lincoln
80. What are the 49th and 50th states of the union?	80. Alaska and Hawaii
81. Who were the United States's enemies in World War II?	81. Germany, Italy, and Japan
82. Who was Martin Luther King, Jr.?	82. a civil rights leader

LA BANDERA

83. What are the colors of our flag?	83. red, white, blue
84. How many stars are on our flag?	84. fifty (50)
85. What color are the stars on our flag?	85. white
86. What do the stars on the flag represent?	86. The fifty (50) states. There is one star for each state in the union.
87. How many stripes are on the flag?	87. thirteen (13)
88. What color are the stripes?	88. red and white
89. What do the stripes on the flag represent?	89. original thirteen (13) colonies

EL GOBIERNO DE TU ESTADO

90. What is the capital of your state?	90. Cada estado tiene una respuesta diferente. Busca cual es la capital del estado en que vives.
91. Who is the current governor of your state?	91. Cada estado tiene una respuesta differente. Busca quien es el gobernador del estado en que vives.
92. Who is the head of your local government?	92. Aprende el nombre de tu alcalde.

93. How many states are there in the United States?

93. fifty (50)

94. Name one purpose of the United Nations.

94. for countries to talk about world problems and try to solve them

95. Name one benefit of becoming a citizen of the United States.

95. right to vote, right to travel with a U.S. passport, right to serve on a jury, right to apply for federal jobs.

96. What are the two major political parties in the U.S. today?

96. Democrat and Republican

97. What kind of government does the U.S. have?

97. Democratic Republic

98. What is the United States Capitol?

98. place where Congress meets

99. Where is the capital of the United States?

99. Washington, DC

100. What INS form is used to apply to become a naturalized citizen?

100. Form N-400 "Application for Naturalization"

CAPÍTULO 7

Preguntas y Respuestas Típicas del Formulario N-400

Estas son muchas de las preguntas, con sus respuestas respectivas, que pueden preguntarte durante la entrevista con el INS o en la solicitud N-400 cuando estés solicitando el formulario. Muchas de las preguntas ya fueron presentadas en las lecciones del capítulo 4. Podrás notar que pocas preguntan lo mismo. Tienes que estar preparado para contestar estas preguntas hechas de distintas maneras. Las palabras marcadas son aquellas para las cuales tú puedes encontrar el significado en el capítulo 5. Practica respondiendo las preguntas usando tu propia información. Haz que alguien lea las preguntas en voz alta y tú las contestes.

Pregunta:	Do you understand what an **oath** is?
Respuesta:	Yes, it is a promise to tell the truth.
Pregunta:	What is your complete name?
Respuesta:	My name is Yolanda Rodriguez Martinez.
Pregunta:	What is your name?
Respuesta:	Yolanda Rodriguez Martinez.
Pregunta:	What is your **address**?
Respuesta:	My address is 423 Tenth Avenue, Brooklyn, New York 11209.
Pregunta:	Where do you live?
Respuesta:	I live at 423 Tenth Avenue, Brooklyn, New York 11209.

Pregunta:	What is your home phone number?
Respuesta:	My home phone number is 718-555-7889.
Pregunta:	What is your telephone number at home?
Respuesta:	It is 718-555-7889.
Pregunta:	Do you have a work telephone number?
Respuesta:	Yes, my work number is 212-555-6000.
Pregunta:	What is your work phone number?
Respuesta:	My work phone number is 212-555-6000.
Pregunta:	Do you have a work number?
Respuesta:	No, I am not currently working.
Pregunta:	May I see your passport?
Respuesta:	Yes, here it is.
Pregunta:	Do you have your passport with you?
Respuesta:	Yes, I do.
Pregunta:	What is your current **citizenship**?
Respuesta:	I am currently a **citizen** of Mexico.
Pregunta:	Your current citizenship is?
Respuesta:	Mexican.
Pregunta:	What is your date of birth?
Respuesta:	I was born on July 12, 1953.
Pregunta:	When were you born?
Respuesta:	On July 12, 1953.
Pregunta:	What is your birth date?
Respuesta:	My birth date is July 12, 1953.
Pregunta:	Where were you born?
Respuesta:	I was born in India.
Pregunta:	What is your place of birth?
Respuesta:	I was born in India.
Pregunta:	What is your **birth place**?
Respuesta:	I was born in India.
Pregunta:	What is your **marital status**?
Respuesta:	I am married.

Pregunta:	What is your **marital status**?
Respuesta:	I am divorced.
Pregunta:	Are you married?
Respuesta:	No, I am single.
Pregunta:	Have you ever been married previously?
Respuesta:	Yes, I was married for one year when I lived in Mexico.
Pregunta:	Is your husband a United States citizen?
Respuesta:	No, he is not a United States citizen.
Pregunta:	Is your wife a United States citizen?
Respuesta:	Yes, she is.
Pregunta:	Why did you get a divorce?
Respuesta:	We fought too much.
Pregunta:	How long have you been married?
Respuesta:	I have been married for ten years.
Pregunta:	How long have you been a Permanent Resident of the United States?
Respuesta:	I have been a resident for ten years.
Pregunta:	When did you first come to the United States?
Respuesta:	I arrived in the United States in 1989.
Pregunta:	On what date did you enter the United States?
Respuesta:	I arrived in the United States on September 5, 1989.
Pregunta:	How long have you lived in the United States?
Respuesta:	I have lived in the United States for ten years.
Pregunta:	Where did you enter the United States?
Respuesta:	I entered the United States in New York City.
Pregunta:	What was your **port of entry**?
Respuesta:	JFK airport in New York City.
Pregunta:	In what **port of entry** did you arrive in America?
Respuesta:	My port of entry was the Los Angeles airport.
Pregunta:	What was your port of entry?
Respuesta:	I crossed the United States border near Seattle, Washington.
Pregunta:	When did you become a Permanent Resident?
Respuesta:	I became a Permanent Resident in 1990.

Pregunta:	In what year did you arrive in the United States?
Respuesta:	I came to America in 1989.
Pregunta:	Who is your **employer**?
Respuesta:	I am unemployed right now.
Pregunta:	Why aren't you working?
Respuesta:	I was laid off from my last job, and I'm looking for a new job.
Pregunta:	Who is your current **employer**?
Respuesta:	My employer is Machines, Inc.
Pregunta:	Who do you currently work for?
Respuesta:	I work for Machines, Inc.
Pregunta:	Are you currently working?
Respuesta:	Yes, I work for Machines, Inc.
Pregunta:	What kind of work do you do?
Respuesta:	I work for Machines, Inc. as a factory worker.
Pregunta:	Do you have a job?
Respuesta:	Yes, I work at Machines, Inc.
Pregunta:	What is your **occupation**?
Respuesta:	I am a factory worker.
Pregunta:	What kind of income do you have?
Respuesta:	I get an income from working for Machines, Inc.
Pregunta:	How do you support yourself?
Respuesta:	I work for Machines, Inc.
Pregunta:	How long have you held this job?
Respuesta:	I have had this job for three years.
Pregunta:	Who was your **employer** before that?
Respuesta:	I used to work for Southwest Airlines.
Pregunta:	What job did you have there?
Respuesta:	I worked as a shipping clerk.
Pregunta:	How many children do you have?
Respuesta:	I have three children.
Pregunta:	Do your children live with you?
Respuesta:	Yes, my children live in my home.

Pregunta: How many people live in your house?
Respuesta: Five people: myself, my husband, and three children.

Pregunta: Who do you live with?
Respuesta: I live with my husband and three children.

Pregunta: Where do your children live?
Respuesta: My children live with me in Brooklyn, New York.

Pregunta: Did any of your children stay in your native country?
Respuesta: No, all of my children live with me here in Brooklyn.

Pregunta: When were your children **born**?
Respuesta: One was born in 1992, one in 1994, and one in 1997.

Pregunta: Were they all born in the United States?
Respuesta: Yes, they were born in America.

Pregunta: How many times have you left the United States since you became a Permanent Resident?
Respuesta: I went out of America only one time.

Pregunta: How long were you away?
Respuesta: I was gone for three weeks.

Pregunta: Where did you go?
Respuesta: I went to visit my aunt in Poland.

Pregunta: Why did you leave the United States?
Respuesta: I wanted to visit my aunt in Poland because she was dying.

Pregunta: Since becoming a Permanent Resident, have you ever left the United States?
Respuesta: I left only once to go visit my grandmother in Mexico.

Pregunta: When was the last time you left the United States?
Respuesta: I went to Canada two years ago.

Pregunta: Have you left the United States since you became a Permanent Resident?
Respuesta: No, I've never left the United States.

Pregunta: Since coming to the U.S., have you traveled to any other country?
Respuesta: No, I've never left the United States.

Pregunta:	Have you visited any other country since becoming a Permanent Resident?
Respuesta:	Yes, I went to Poland to visit my aunt one time.
Pregunta:	Have you ever been **deported** by the Immigration office?
Respuesta:	No, I have never been ordered to leave America.
Pregunta:	Were you ever ordered to leave the United States?
Respuesta:	No, I have never been **deported**.
Pregunta:	Have you ever used a **different** name?
Respuesta:	Yes, my last name used to be Alloutuseth.
Pregunta:	Do you want to change your name?
Respuesta:	Yes, I want to change my last name to Allseth.
Pregunta:	What other names have you gone by?
Respuesta:	I used to be called Massouleh Alloutuseth.
Pregunta:	To what do you want to change your name?
Respuesta:	I want my new name to be Sue Allseth.
Pregunta:	What name do you want to have now?
Respuesta:	Sue Allseth.
Pregunta:	How do you spell that?
Respuesta:	S-u-e A-l-l-s-e-t-h.
Pregunta:	What other names have you used in the past?
Respuesta:	I've never used any other names.
Pregunta:	What was your **maiden name**?
Respuesta:	Before I was married, my name was Massouleh Tomei.
Pregunta:	What other names have you used in the past?
Respuesta:	Before I was married my name was Massouleh Tomei.
Pregunta:	When did you change your name?
Respuesta:	I changed my name ten years ago when I was married.
Pregunta:	Why do you want to be an American citizen?
Respuesta:	I want to vote.
Pregunta:	Why do you want to be a U.S. citizen?
Respuesta:	I want to travel with a U.S. passport.
Pregunta:	Why have you applied for naturalization?
Respuesta:	I want to bring my mother to America.

Pregunta:	Were you ever **arrested**?
Respuesta:	Yes, a long time ago.
Pregunta:	What were you **arrested** for?
Respuesta:	I stole some money from the corner store.
Pregunta:	How about any other arrests?
Respuesta:	No, that was the only time I was **arrested**.
Pregunta:	Have you ever committed any crime for which you have not been arrested?
Respuesta:	No, I've never done any crimes that I wasn't punished for.
Pregunta:	Have you ever been imprisoned for breaking any law?
Respuesta:	I was in jail for three months for robbing the corner store.
Pregunta:	When was that?
Respuesta:	During the winter of 1989.
Pregunta:	Have you ever failed to file a federal **income tax** return?
Respuesta:	No, I have always filed my taxes.
Pregunta:	Have you filed your federal taxes every year?
Respuesta:	Yes, I pay my taxes every year.
Pregunta:	Do you pay taxes?
Respuesta:	Yes, I pay federal and state taxes each year.
Pregunta:	Was there ever a year when you didn't file your federal tax forms?
Respuesta:	No, I've filed my tax forms every year since I came to America.
Pregunta:	Was there ever a year when you didn't file your federal tax forms?
Respuesta:	Yes, I didn't file my first two years in America because I made no money.
Pregunta:	Do you pay taxes?
Respuesta:	No, I don't have a job so I don't pay federal income taxes.
Pregunta:	Have you ever been a **habitual drunkard**?
Respuesta:	No, I drink only a little.
Pregunta:	Were you ever drunk every day?
Respuesta:	No, I drink only one glass of wine a week.

Pregunta: Have you ever advocated or practiced **polygamy**?
Respuesta: No, I have only one wife.

Pregunta: Have you ever been married to more than one person at a time?
Respuesta: No, I have always had only one husband.

Pregunta: Have you ever practiced **polygamy**?
Respuesta: No, I am not married, and I have never been married.

Pregunta: Have you ever been a **prostitute**?
Respuesta: No, I don't sell my body.

Pregunta: Have you ever been a **prostitute**?
Respuesta: No, I've never taken money for sex.

Pregunta: Have you ever sold your body for money?
Respuesta: No, I've never been a **prostitute**.

Pregunta: Have you ever knowingly and for gain helped any alien to enter the U.S. illegally?
Respuesta: No, I have never **smuggled** anyone into the country.

Pregunta: Have you ever helped someone enter the U.S. illegally?
Respuesta: No, I have never **smuggled** anyone into the country.

Pregunta: Have you ever **smuggled** anyone into the U.S.?
Respuesta: No, I have never helped anyone enter America illegally.

Pregunta: Have you ever accepted money for sneaking someone into the U.S.?
Respuesta: No, I have never helped anyone enter America illegally.

Pregunta: Have you ever been a trafficker in **illegal drugs**?
Respuesta: No, I have never touched **illegal drugs**.

Pregunta: Have you ever bought or sold **illegal drugs**?
Respuesta: No, I am not a drug trafficker.

Pregunta: Have you ever carried **illegal drugs** for someone else?
Respuesta: No, I have never handled **illegal drugs**.

Pregunta: Have you ever bought or sold **illegal drugs**?
Respuesta: No, I have never purchased or sold **illegal drugs**.

Pregunta: Have you ever received income from **illegal gambling**?
Respuesta: No, I don't gamble.

Pregunta:	Did you ever get money illegally from gambling?
Respuesta:	No, I don't gamble for money.
Pregunta:	Have you ever received money from **illegal gambling**?
Respuesta:	No, I don't gamble for money.
Pregunta:	Have you ever received money or other goods from **illegal gambling**?
Respuesta:	No, I don't bet on anything.
Pregunta:	Have you ever claimed in writing or in any other way to be a U.S. citizen?
Respuesta:	No, I have never lied about my status.
Pregunta:	Have you ever **claimed** in writing or in any other way to be a U.S. citizen?
Respuesta:	No, I never said I was a U.S. citizen.
Pregunta:	Have you ever pretended to be a U.S. citizen?
Respuesta:	No, I have never lied about my citizenship.
Pregunta:	Have you ever **claimed** in writing to be a U.S. citizen?
Respuesta:	No, I have never pretended to be an American citizen.
Pregunta:	Have you ever claimed in writing or in any other way to be a U.S. citizen?
Respuesta:	No, I am not a U.S. citizen.
Pregunta:	Have you ever voted or **registered** to vote in the United States?
Respuesta:	No, I have never tried to vote because I am not a U.S. citizen.
Pregunta:	Have you ever voted or **registered** to vote in the United States?
Respuesta:	No, I am not a U.S. citizen.
Pregunta:	Have you ever voted or **registered** to vote in the United States?
Respuesta:	No, I have never tried to vote in America.
Pregunta:	Do you believe in the **Constitution** and the government of the United States?
Respuesta:	Yes, I think the **Constitution** is a good law.
Pregunta:	Do you believe in the **Constitution** of the United States?
Respuesta:	Yes, I want to follow the **Constitution**.

Pregunta:	Do you believe in the government of the United States?
Respuesta:	Yes, I think the government is very good.
Pregunta:	Do you believe in the **Constitution** and the government of the United States?
Respuesta:	Yes, I believe that the **Constitution** is a good law.
Pregunta:	Are you willing to take the full **Oath of Allegiance** to the United States?
Respuesta:	Yes, I am ready to help my new country.
Pregunta:	Are you willing to take the full **Oath of Allegiance** to the United States?
Respuesta:	Yes, I promise to help my new country. I can't help my old country.
Pregunta:	Are you willing to take the full **Oath of Allegiance** to the United States?
Respuesta:	Yes, I want to do what is best for America.
Pregunta:	Are you willing to take the full **Oath of Allegiance** to the United States?
Respuesta:	Yes, I want to officially swear to help the United States.
Pregunta:	Have you ever been declared legally **incompetent** or confined as a patient in a **mental institution**?
Respuesta:	No, I am not crazy.
Pregunta:	Were you ever in a mental hospital?
Respuesta:	No, I am mentally competent.
Pregunta:	Have you ever been confined as a patient in a **mental institution**?
Respuesta:	No, I've never been in a hospital for people whose minds don't work right.
Pregunta:	Were you born with or have you acquired any title of **nobility**?
Respuesta:	No, my parents were factory workers.
Pregunta:	Are you a king, queen, duke, earl, prince, or do you have any other title of **nobility**?
Respuesta:	No, I don't have any special titles along with my name and I am not a king or any other noble.

Pregunta:	Were you born with or have you acquired any title of **nobility**?
Respuesta:	No, no one in my family is related to a king or queen.
Pregunta:	Have you at any time ever ordered, incited, assisted, or otherwise participated in the **persecution** of any person because of race, religion, national origin, or political opinion?
Respuesta:	No, I have never hurt anyone.
Pregunta:	Have you at any time ever ordered or otherwise participated in the **persecution** of any person because of race, religion, national origin, or political opinion?
Respuesta:	No, I don't hurt people because of what they believe or what color they are.
Pregunta:	Have you ever participated in the **persecution** of any person because of race, religion, national origin, or political opinion?
Respuesta:	No, I have never persecuted anyone.
Pregunta:	If the law requires it, are you willing to perform **noncombatant services** in the Armed Forces of the United States?
Respuesta:	Yes, I will help the soldiers when the law tells me.
Pregunta:	If required by law, are you willing to perform **noncombatant services** in the Armed Forces of the United States?
Respuesta:	Yes, I will do whatever I can to help the military.
Pregunta:	Are you willing to perform **noncombatant services** in the Armed Forces of the United States, if the law says you must?
Respuesta:	Yes, I will help the Armed Forces if the law tells me.
Pregunta:	If the law requires it, are you willing to perform work of **national importance** under civilian direction?
Respuesta:	Yes, I will do anything to help the United States when the law says I must.
Pregunta:	Are you willing to perform work of **national importance** under civilian direction, if required by the law?
Respuesta:	Yes, if the law tells me, I will work to help the United States.
Pregunta:	Will you perform work of **national importance** under civilian direction, when the law says you must?
Respuesta:	Yes, I will do anything to help the United States whenever it is needed.

Pregunta:	Have you ever left the United States to avoid being **drafted** into the U.S. Armed Forces?
Respuesta:	No, I have never gone away to avoid going into the military.
Pregunta:	Have you ever left the United States to avoid being **drafted**?
Respuesta:	No, I have never left the country so I didn't have to go to war.
Pregunta:	Have you ever left the United States so you didn't have to fight in a war?
Respuesta:	No, I have never gone away to avoid being **drafted** into the military.
Pregunta:	Have you ever failed to comply with **Selective Service** laws?
Respuesta:	No, I never withheld my name for becoming a soldier.
Pregunta:	Have you ever failed to comply with **Selective Service** laws?
Respuesta:	No, I have always given my name so I could be called to fight.
Pregunta:	Did you register for the **Selective Service**?
Respuesta:	Yes, I gave my name to the government.
Pregunta:	Do you know your **Selective Service** number?
Respuesta:	Yes, I have that number written on this paper.
Pregunta:	Did you ever apply for **exemption** from military service because of alienage, **conscientious objections**, or other reasons?
Respuesta:	No, I have never said that I would not fight for America.
Pregunta:	Have you ever tried to avoid military service?
Respuesta:	No, I have always been willing to be a soldier.
Pregunta:	Did you ever request to stay out of the Armed Forces because of your religious beliefs?
Respuesta:	No, my religion says it is okay to protect my country by fighting a war.
Pregunta:	Have you ever **deserted** from the military, air, or naval forces of the United States?
Respuesta:	No, I have never even been in the Armed Forces.
Pregunta:	Have you ever **deserted** from the military, air, or naval forces of the United States?
Respuesta:	No, I was honorably discharged from the army.

Pregunta:	Did you leave the Armed Forces before you were allowed to?
Respuesta:	No, I was in the Armed Forces for a full three years.
Pregunta:	Are you a member of the **Communist** Party?
Respuesta:	No, I am not a member of any group.
Pregunta:	Have you ever been a member of the **Communist** Party?
Respuesta:	No, I never joined that group.
Pregunta:	Are you now or have you ever been a member of the **Communist** Party?
Respuesta:	I am not a member now, but I was many years ago.
Pregunta:	Why were you a **Communist**?
Respuesta:	I joined because everyone else joined. I didn't believe in it.
Pregunta:	When was that?
Respuesta:	I joined in 1972, but I never went to the meetings.
Pregunta:	Have you ever been **affiliated** with the Nazi Party?
Respuesta:	No, I don't agree with the Nazi Party.
Pregunta:	Have you ever been a member of the Nazi Party?
Respuesta:	No, I never joined the Nazi Party.
Pregunta:	Did you help the Nazi government in any way?
Respuesta:	No, I never assisted the Nazis.
Pregunta:	Were you a part of the Nazi Party between 1933 and 1945?
Respuesta:	No, I don't agree with the Nazi Party.
Pregunta:	Have you ever helped the Nazi Party?
Respuesta:	No, I don't like the Nazi Party.
Pregunta:	Are you a member of any clubs or organizations?
Respuesta:	No, I am not a part of any organized groups.
Pregunta:	Are you a member of any clubs or organizations?
Respuesta:	Yes, I am a member of the Small Business Association.
Pregunta:	Are you a member of any clubs?
Respuesta:	No, I do not take part in any clubs.
Pregunta:	Have you ever given **false testimony** to obtain an immigration benefit?
Respuesta:	No, I have never lied.

Pregunta:	Have you ever lied to obtain an immigration benefit?
Respuesta:	No, I have never given **false testimony**.
Pregunta:	Have you ever lied at an immigration interview when you were under **oath**?
Respuesta:	No, I have never lied after swearing to tell the truth.
Pregunta:	If the law requires it, are you willing to bear arms on behalf of the United States?
Respuesta:	Yes, I will fight in a war to help the United States.
Pregunta:	If the law requires it, are you willing to **bear arms** on behalf of the United States?
Respuesta:	Yes, I will be a soldier if the law tells me.
Pregunta:	Are you willing to **bear arms** for the United States, even if it is against the country you used to live in?
Respuesta:	Yes, I will fight for America even if it is against my old country.

CAPÍTULO 8

Ejemplos de Oraciones de Dictado

Estos son ejemplos de oraciones que pueden pedirte que escribas durante tu entrevista con el INS. Estas oraciones de dictado fueron presentadas anteriormente en las lecciones del Capítulo 4. Haz que alguien te las lea en voz alta y escríbelas cuidadosamente.

1. I study.
2. I study English.
3. I study citizenship.
4. I want to be a citizen.
5. I want to be an American.
6. I live in California.
7. I live with my family.
8. I live in California with my family.
9. I want to be an American citizen.
10. I want to be a citizen of the United States.
11. I drive to work.
12. I drive my car to work.
13. I like to drive my car to work.
14. I take the bus.
15. I take the bus to work.
16. I like to take the bus.
17. I go to school.
18. My children go to school.

1. _____

2. _____

3. _____

4. _____

5. _____

6. _____

7. _____

8. _____

9. _____

10. _____

11. _____

12. _____

13. _____

14. _____

15. _____

16. _____

17. _____

18. _____

19. My children and I go to school.

20. The little girl is happy.

21. My family is happy to be in America.

22. The little girl and my family are happy.

23. I believe in freedom.

24. I believe in the Constitution.

25. I believe in freedom and the Constitution.

26. The sky is blue.

27. My dog is brown.

28. The sky is blue and my dog is brown.

29. There is a bird.

30. The bird is in the tree.

31. There is a bird in the tree.

32. I have four children.

33. I live with my children.

34. I live with my four children.

35. I drive a car.

36. I drive a big red car.

19. _____

20. _____

21. _____

22. _____

23. _____

24. _____

25. _____

26. _____

27. _____

28. _____

29. _____

30. _____

31. _____

32. _____

33. _____

34. _____

35. _____

36. _____

37. I like my car.

38. I live in a house.

39. I live in a blue house.

40. I like my house.

41. The woman eats.

42. The woman eats food.

43. The woman eats two apples.

44. I have a cat.

45. I have a small cat.

46. I like cats.

47. I wear a hat.

48. I wear a yellow hat.

49. I wear hats.

50. I am learning English.

51. They are learning English.

52. My sisters are learning English.

53. I like snow.

54. Today it is snowing.

37. _____

38. _____

39. _____

40. _____

41. _____

42. _____

43. _____

44. _____

45. _____

46. _____

47. _____

48. _____

49. _____

50. _____

51. _____

52. _____

53. _____

54. _____

55. The snow is cold.

56. The child plays.

57. The child plays with a toy.

58. The child likes the toy.

59. I can read English.

60. I can write English.

61. I can read, write, and speak English.

62. Today is Tuesday.

63. Tomorrow is Wednesday.

64. Today it is windy.

65. It is cold.

66. It is cold outside.

67. I like cold weather.

55. _____

56. _____

57. _____

58. _____

59. _____

60. _____

61. _____

62. _____

63. _____

64. _____

65. _____

66. _____

67. _____

APÉNDICE A

INFORMACIÓN DE CONTACTO

CÓMO PONERSE EN CONTACTO CON EL INS

Telefono: **1-800-375-5283**
TTY: **1-800-767-1833**
Sitio web: www.ins.usdoj.gov

OFICINAS DEL INS POR ESTADO

ALABAMA
Atlanta, Georgia District Office
Martin Luther King Jr. Federal Building
77 Forsyth Street SW
Atlanta, GA 30303

ALASKA
Anchorage
620 East 10th Avenue
Suite 102
Anchorage, AL 99501

ARIZONA
Phoenix
2035 N. Central Avenue
Phoenix, AZ 85004

Tucson
6431 South Country Club Road
Tucson, AZ 85706-5907
(Sub-office serving Cochise, Pima, Santa
   Cruz, Graham and Pinal)

ARKANSAS
Fort Smith
4991 Old Greenwood Road
Fort Smith, AR 72903
(Sub-office serving western Arkansas. The
   district office is located in New Orleans)

CALIFORNIA
Los Angeles
300 North Los Angeles Street
Room 1001
Los Angeles, CA 90012
(District office serving Los Angeles, Orange,
   Riverside, San Bernardino, Santa Barbara,
   San Luis Obispo and Ventura counties.
   There are also offices in East Los Angeles,
   El Monte, Bell, Bellflower, Westminster,
   Santa Ana, Camarillo, Riverside, San
   Pedro, Los Angeles International Airport,
   Lompoc, and Lancaster)

San Diego
880 Front Street
Suite 1234
San Diego, CA 92101
(District office serving San Diego and
    Imperial counties)

San Francisco
444 Washington Street
San Francisco, CA 94111
(District office serving Alameda, Contra
    Costa, Del Norte, Glenn, Humboldt, Lake,
    Lassen, Marin, Mendocino, Modoc, Napa,
    San Francisco, San Mateo, Shasta,
    Siskiyou, Solano, Sonoma, Stanislaus,
    Tehama, and Trinity)

Fresno
865 Fulton Mall
Fresno, CA 93721
(Sub-office serving Fresno, Inyo, Kern,
    Kings, Madera, Mariposa, Merced, Mono,
    and Tulare)

Sacramento
650 Capitol Mall
Sacramento, CA 95814
(Sub-office serving Alpine, Amador, Butte,
    Calaveras, Colusa, El Dorado, Nevada,
    Placer, Plumas, Sacramento, San Joaquin,
    Sierra, Sutter, Tuolumne, Yolo and Yuba)

San Jose
1887 Monterey Road
San Jose, CA 95112
(Sub-office serving Monterey, San Benito,
    Santa Clara and Santa Cruz)

COLORADO
Denver
4730 Paris Street
Denver, CO 80239

CONNECTICUT
Hartford
450 Main Street
4th Floor
Hartford, CT 06103-3060
(Sub-office serving Connecticut. The district
    office is located in Boston.)

WASHINGTON DC
4420 N. Fairfax Drive
Arlington, VA 22203
(District office serving the entire state of
    Virginia and the District of Columbia)

DELAWARE
Dover
1305 McD Drive
Dover, DE 19901
(Satellite office, district office is in
    Philadelphia)

FLORIDA
Miami
7880 Biscayne Boulevard
Miami, FL 33138
(District Office)

Jacksonville
4121 Southpoint Boulevard
Jacksonville, FL 32216
(Sub-office serving Alachua, Baker, Bay,
    Bradford, Calhoun, Clay, Columbia, Dixie,
    Duval, Escambia, Franklin, Gadsden,
    Gilchrist, Gulf, Hamilton, Holmes, Jackson,
    Jefferson, Lafayette, Leon, Levy, Liberty,
    Madison, Nassau, Okaloosa, Putnum,
    Santa Rosa, St. Johns, Suwanee, Taylor,
    Union, Wakulla, Walton, and Washington)

Orlando
9403 Tradeport Drive
Orlando, FL 32827
(Sub-office serving Orange, Osceola,
    Seminole, Lake, Brevard, Flagler, Volusia,
    Marion, and Sumter)

Tampa
5524 West Cypress Street
Tampa, FL 33607-1708
(Sub-office serving Citrus, Hernando, Pasco,
  Pinellas, Hillsborough, Polk, Hardee,
  Manatee, Sarasota, De Soto, Charlotte,
  and Lee)

West Palm Beach
301 Broadway
Riviera Beach, FL 33404
(Sub-office serving Palm Beach, Martin, St.
  Lucie, Indian River, Okeechobee, Hendry,
  Glades, and Highland counties in Florida)

GEORGIA
Atlanta
Martin Luther King Jr. Federal Building
77 Forsyth Street SW
Atlanta, GA 30303

GUAM
Agana
Sirena Plaza
108 Hernan Cortez Avenue
Suite 801
Hagatna, Guam 96910
(Sub-office serving Guam and the Northern
  Mariana Islands, district office is located in
  Honolulu)

HAWAII
Honolulu
595 Ala Moana Boulevard
Honolulu, HI 96813
(District office serving Hawaii, the Territory of
  Guam, and The Commonwealth of
  Northern Marianas)

IDAHO
Boise
4620 Overland Road
Room 108
Boise, ID 83705
(Sub-office serving southwest and South
  Central Idaho, district office is located in
  Helena, Montana)

ILLINOIS
Chicago
10 West Jackson Boulevard
Chicago, IL 60604

INDIANA
Indianapolis
950 N. Meridian St.
Room 400
Indianapolis, IN 46204
(Sub-office serving the State of Indiana
  except Lake, Porter, LaPorte, and St.
  Joseph counties in Northwest Indiana.
  Residents of those four counties are
  served by The Chicago District Office.)

IOWA
Des Moines
210 Walnut Street
Room 369
Des Moines, IA 50302
(Satellite office, district office is located in
  Omaha, Nebraska.)

KANSAS
Wichita
271 West 3rd Street North
Suite 1050
Wichita, KS 67202-1212
(Satellite office serving western Kansas, dis-
  trict office is located in Kansas City,
  Missouri)

KENTUCKY
Louisville
Gene Snyder U.S. Courthouse and
Customhouse
Room 390
601 West Broadway
Louisville, KY 40202
(Sub-office serving Kentucky and parts of
  eastern Tennessee)

LOUISIANA
New Orleans
701 Loyola Avenue
New Orleans, LA 70113
(Serving Louisiana and southern Mississippi)

MAINE
Portland
176 Gannett Drive
Portland, ME 04106
(Serving Maine and Vermont)

MARYLAND
Baltimore
George H. Fallon Federal Building
31 Hopkins Plaza
Baltimore, MD 21201

MASSACHUSETTS
Boston
John F. Kennedy Federal Building
Government Center
Boston, MA 02203

MICHIGAN
Detroit
333 Mt. Elliott
Detroit, MI 48207

MINNESOTA
St. Paul
2901 Metro Drive
Suite 100
Bloomington, MN 55425
(Serving Minnesota, North Dakota, and South
Dakota)

MISSISSIPPI
Jackson
Dr. A. H. McCoy Federal Building
100 West Capitol Street
Suite B-8
Jackson, Mississippi 39269
(Sub-office serving Mississippi, district office
is located in New Orleans)

MISSOURI
Kansas City
9747 Northwest Conant Avenue
Kansas City, MO 64153
(District office serving western Missouri and
eastern Kansas)

St. Louis
Robert A. Young Building
1222 Spruce Street
Room 1.100
St. Louis, Missouri
(Sub-office serving eastern part of Missouri)

MONTANA
Helena
2800 Skyway Drive
Helena, MT 59602
(District office for Montana and northern por-
tions of Idaho)

NEBRASKA
Omaha
3736 South 132nd Street
West Omaha, NE 68144
(District office serving Nebraska and Iowa)

NEW JERSEY
Newark
970 Broad Street
Newark, NJ 07102
(District office serving Bergen, Essex,
Hudson, Hunterdon, Middlesex, Morris,
Passaic, Somerset, Sussex, Union, and
Warren Counties)

Cherry Hill
1886 Greentree Road
Cherry Hill, NJ 08003
(Sub-office serving Atlantic, Burlington,
Camden, Cape May, Cumberland,
Gloucester, Mercer, Monmouth, Ocean,
and Salem)

NEW MEXICO
Albuquerque
1720 Randolph Road SE
Albuquerque, NM 87106
(Sub-office serving northern New Mexico,
district office is located in El Paso, Texas)

PASE EL EXAMEN DE CIUDADANÍA AMERICANA

NEW YORK
Buffalo
Federal Center
130 Delaware Avenue
Buffalo, NY 14202
(District office serving the state of New York,
  with the exception of New York City and its
  surrounding counties)

New York City
26 Federal Plaza
New York, NY 10278
(District office serving the five boroughs of
  NYC, Richmond, Nassau, Suffolk,
  Dutchess, Orange, Putnam, Rockland,
  Sullivan, Ulster, and Westchester counties)

Albany
1086 Troy-Schenectady Road
Latham, NY 12110
(Sub-office serving Albany, Broome,
  Chenango, Clinton, Columbia, Delaware,
  Essex, Franklin, Fulton, Greene, Hamilton,
  Herkimer, Madison, Montgomery, Oneida,
  Otsego, Rensselaer, Saint Lawrence,
  Saratoga, Schenectady, Schoharie, Tioga,
  Warren, and Washington counties)

NORTH CAROLINA
Charlotte
210 East Woodlawn Road
Building 6, Suite 138
Charlotte, NC 28217
(Sub-office serving North Carolina, district
  office is located in Atlanta)

NORTH DAKOTA
St. Paul, Minnesota District Office
2901 Metro Drive
Suite 100
Bloomington, MN 55425
(District office serving North Dakota, South
  Dakota, and Minnesota)

OHIO
Cleveland
AJC Federal Building
1240 East Ninth Street
Room 1917
Cleveland, OH 44199
(District office serving the northern part of
  Ohio)

Cincinnati
J.W. Peck Federal Building
550 Main Street
Room 4001
Cincinnati, OH 45202
(Sub-office serving the southern part of Ohio)

OKLAHOMA
Oklahoma City
4149 Highline Boulevard
Suite #300
Oklahoma City, OK 73108-2081
(Sub-office serving Oklahoma, district office
  is located in Dallas)

OREGON
Portland
511 NW Broadway
Portland, OR 97209
(District office serving Oregon)

PENNSYLVANIA
Philadelphia
1600 Callowhill Street
Philadelphia, PA 19130
(District office for Pennsylvania, Delaware,
  and West Virginia)

Pittsburgh
1000 Liberty Avenue
Federal Building
Room 2130
Pittsburgh, PA 15222-4181
(Sub-office serving western Pennsylvania
  and West Virginia)

PUERTO RICO
San Juan
San Patricio Office Center
7 Tabonuco Street
Suite 100
Guaynabo, PR 00936
(District office serving Puerto Rico and the
U.S. Virgin Islands)

RHODE ISLAND
Providence
200 Dyer Street
Providence, RI 02903
(Sub-office serving Rhode Island)

SOUTH CAROLINA
Charleston
142-D West Phillips Road
Greer, SC 29650
(Sub-office serving South Carolina, district
office is located in Atlanta)

SOUTH DAKOTA
St. Paul, Minnesota District Office
2901 Metro Drive
Suite 100
Bloomington, MN 55425
(District office serving South Dakota, North
Dakota, and Minnesota)

TENNESSEE*
Memphis
1341 Sycamore View Road
Memphis, TN 38134
(Sub-office serving the eastern half of
Arkansas, the top half of Mississippi, and
the State of Tennessee, district office is
located in New Orleans)
*(Naturalization cases in Anderson, Bedford,
Bledsoe, Blount, Bradley, Campbell, Carter,
Claiborne, Cocke, Coffee, Franklin, Grainger,
Greene, Grundy, Hamblen, Hamilton,
Hancock, Hawkins, Jefferson, Johnson,
Knox, Lincoln, Loudon, Marion, McMinn,
Meigs, Monroe, Moore, Morgan, Polk, Rhea,
Roane, Scott, Sequatchie, Sevier, Sullivan,
Unicoi, Union, Van Buren, Warren, and
Washington counties fall under the jurisdic-
tion of the Louisville, Kentucky sub-office)*

TEXAS
Dallas
8101 North Stemmons Freeway
Dallas, TX 75247
(District office serving 123 northern counties
in the State of Texas and all of Oklahoma)

El Paso
1545 Hawkins Boulevard
El Paso, TX 79925
(District office serving West Texas and New
Mexico)

Harlingen
2102 Teege Avenue
Harlingen, TX 78550
(District office serving Brooks, Cameron,
Hidalgo, Kennedy, Kleberg, Starr, and
Willacy)

Houston
126 Northpoint
Houston, TX 77060
(District office serving southeastern Texas)

San Antonio
8940 Fourwinds Drive
San Antonio, TX 78239
(District office serving Central and South
Texas)

UTAH
Salt Lake City
5272 South College Drive, #100
Murray, UT 84123
(Sub-office serving Utah, district office is
located in Denver)

VERMONT
St. Albans
64 Gricebrook Road
St. Albans, VT 05478
(Sub-office serving Vermont and New
Hampshire, district office is located in
Portland, Maine)

US VIRGIN ISLANDS
Charlotte Amalie
Nisky Center
Suite 1A First Floor South
Charlotte Amalie,
St. Thomas, USVI 00802
(Sub-office serving St. Thomas and St. John, district office is located in San Juan)

St. Croix
Sunny Isle Shopping Center
Christiansted
St. Croix, USVI 00820
(Sub-office serving St. Croix, U.S. Virgin Islands, district office is located in San Juan)

VIRGINIA
Norfolk
5280 Henneman Drive
Norfolk, Virginia 23513
(Sub-office serving southeastern Virginia, district office is located in Washington DC)

WASHINGTON
Seattle
815 Airport Way South
Seattle WA 98134
(District office serving Washington, and 10 northern counties in Idaho)

Spokane
U.S. Courthouse
920 West Riverside
Room 691
Spokane, WA 99201
(Sub-office serving Adams, Chelan, Asotin, Columbia, Douglas, Ferry, Garfield, Grant, Lincoln, Okanogan, Pend O'reille, Spokane, Stevens, Walla Walla, and Whitman)

Yakima
417 East Chestnut
Yakima, WA 98901
(Sub-office serving Benton, Franklin, Kittitas, Klickitat, and Yakima)

WISCONSIN
Milwaukee
517 East Wisconsin Avenue
Milwaukee, WI 53202
(Sub-office serving Wisconsin, district office is located in Chicago)

International Embassies in the United States
The Argentine Republic
1600 New Hampshire Avenue NW
Washington, DC 20009
Tel: 202-238-6400
Fax: 202-332-3171
www.embassyofargentina-usa.org

Bolivia
3014 Massachusetts Avenue NW
Washington, DC 20008
Tel: 202-483-4410
Fax: 202-328-3712

Brazil
3006 Massachusetts Avenue, NW
Washington, DC 20008
Tel: 202-238-2700
Fax: 202-238-2827
www.brasilemb.org

Chile
1732 Massachusetts Avenue NW
Washington, DC 20036
Tel: 202-785-1746
Fax: 202-887-5579
www.chile-usa.org

The Embassy of Columbia
2118 Leroy Place NW
Washington, DC 20008
Tel: 202-387-8338
Fax: 202-232-8643

Embassy of Costa Rica
2114 "S" Street NW
Washington, DC 20008
Tel: 202-234-2945
www.costarica.com

Cuba Interests Section
2630 and 2639 16th Street NW
Washington, DC 20009
Tel: 202-797-8518
Fax: 202-986-7283

Dominican Republic
1715 22nd. St., NW
Washington, DC 20008

The Embassy of Ecuador
2535 15th Street, NW
Washington, DC 20009
Tel: 202-234-7200
Fax: 202-667-3482

El Salvador
2308 California Street, NW
Washington, DC 20008
Tel: 202-265-9671
www.elsalvador.org

Equatorial Guinea
2020 16th Street, NW
Washington, DC 20009
Tel: 202-518-5700
Fax: 202-518-5252

Guatemala
2220 R Street, NW, Washington, DC 20008
Tel: 202-745-4952
Fax: 202-745-1908
www.mdngt.org/agremilusa/embassy.html

Honduras
3007 Tilden Street, NW
Suite 4M
Washington, DC 20008
Tel: 202-966-7702
Fax: 202-966-9751
www.hondurasemb.org

Mexico
1911 Pennsylvania Avenue, NW
Washington, DC 20006
Tel: 202-728-1600
Fax: 202-728-1698
www.embassyofmexico.org

Nicaragua
1627 New Hampshire Avenue, NW
Washington, DC 20009
Tel: 202-939-6570
Fax: 202-939-6542

The Republic of Panama
2862 McGill Terrace, NW
Washington, DC 20008
Tel: 202-483-1407

Paraguay
2400 Massachusetts Avenue, NW
Washington, DC 20008
Tel: 202-483-6960
Fax: 202-234-4508

Embassy of Peru
1700 Mass. Ave, NW
Washington, DC, 20036
Tel: 202-833-9860
Fax: 202-659-8124
peru@peruemb.org

Embassy of Spain
2375 Pennsylvania Av. NW
Washington, D.C. 20037
Tel: 202-452-0100

Embassy of Uruguay
2715 M St. N.W, 3rd Floor
Washington D.C. 20007
Tel: 202-331-1313
www.embassy.org/uruguay

The Embassy of Venezuela
1099 30th St., N.W.
Washington D.C. 20007
Tel: 202-342 2214
Fax: 202-342 6820
www.embavenez-us.org

APÉNDICE B

RECURSOS EN TU COMUNIDAD

Esos son grupos que ayudan inmigrantes en los Estados Unidos.

Ayuda, Inc.
1736 Columbia Road, NW
Washington, D.C. 20009
Teléfono: 202-387-4848
Fax: 202-387-0324
Sitio web: www.ayudainc.org

American Immigration Lawyers Association
918 F Street, NW
Washington, DC 20004-1400
Teléfono: 202/216-2400
Fax: 202/371-9449
Sitio web: www.aila.org

Catholic Charities USA
1731 King Street, Suite 200
Alexandria, VA 22314
Teléfono: 703-549-1390
Fax: 703-549-1656
Sitio web: www.catholiccharitiesusa.org

Citizenship NYC
Teléfono: 888-374-5100
Sitio web: www.nyc.gov/html/dycd/html/cnyc.html

Colombian American Service Association (C.A.S.A.)
3138 Coral Way
Miami, FL 33145
Teléfono: 305-448-2272
Fax: 305-448-0178
Sitio web: www.casa-usa.org

League of United Latin American Citizens Foundation (LULAC)
1601 Matamoros Street
P.O. Box 880
Laredo, TX 78042-0880
Teléfono: 956-722-5544
Fax: 956-722-7731
Sitio web: www.lulac.org

Los Angeles Unified School District Division of Adult and Career Education
P.O. Box 513307
Los Angeles, CA 90051
Teléfono: 213-625-3276
Sitio web: www.lausd.k12.ca.us

Lutheran Immigration and Refugee Service
(National Headquarters)
700 Light Street
Baltimore MD 21230
Telefono: 410-230-2700
Fax: 410-230-2890
Sitio web: www.lirs.org

Maryland Office for New Americans (MONA)
Department of Human Resources
311 W. Saratoga Street, Room 222
Baltimore, MD 21201
Telefono: 410-767-7514
Sitio web: www.dhr.state.md.us/mona.htm

The Commonwealth of Massachusetts Office for Refugees and Immigrants
18 Tremont Street, Suite 600
Boston, MA 02108
Telefono: 617-727-7888
Fax: 617-727-1822
TTY: 617-727-8149
Sitio web: www.state.ma.us/ori/
   ORI-homepage.html

Naturalization Services Program Department of Community Services and Development
P.O. Box 1947
Sacramento, CA 95814
Telefono: 916-322-2940
Fax: 916- 319-5001
Sitio web: www.csd.ca.gov/Naturalization.htm

New Americans of Washington
615 Market Street, Suite G
Kirkland, WA 98052
Telefono: 425-822-2523
Fax: 425-822-2592
Sitio web: www.newamericans.com

New York Association for New Americans, Inc.
17 Battery Place
New York, NY 10004-1102
Tel. 212-425-2900
Sitio web: www.nyana.org

Services, Immigrant Rights, and Education Network (SIREN)
778 North First Street, Suite 202
San Jose, CA 95112
Telefono: 408-286-5680, x104
Vietnamese Q&A:408-286-1448
Sitio web: www.siren-bayarea.org

St. Anselm's Cross-Cultural Community Center
13091 Galway Street
Garden Grove, CA 92844
Telefono: 714-537-0608
Fax: 714-537-7606
Sitio web: www.saintanselmgg.org

Office of Migration & Refugee Services United States Conference of Catholic Bishops
3211 4th Street, N.E.,
Washington, DC 20017-1194
Telefono: 202-541-3000
Sitio web: www.nccbuscc.org

APÉNDICE C

EJEMPLO DE LA SOLICITUD DEL N-400

U.S. Department of Justice
Immigration and Naturalization Service

OMB No. 1115-0009

Application for Naturalization

Print clearly or type your answers using CAPITAL letters. Failure to print clearly may delay your application. Use black or blue ink.

Part 1. Your Name *(The Person Applying for Naturalization)*

Write your INS "A"- number here:

A _ _ _ _ _ _ _ _ _

A. Your current legal name.

Family Name *(Last Name)*

Given Name *(First Name)*   Full Middle Name *(If applicable)*

B. Your name <u>exactly</u> as it appears on your Permanent Resident Card.

Family Name *(Last Name)*

Given Name *(First Name)*   Full Middle Name *(If applicable)*

C. If you have ever used other names, provide them below.

Family Name *(Last Name)*	Given Name *(First Name)*	Middle Name

D. Name change *(optional)*

Please read the Instructions before you decide whether to change your name.

1. Would you like to legally change your name? ☐ Yes ☐ No

2. If "Yes," print the new name you would like to use. Do not use initials or abbreviations when writing your new name.

Family Name *(Last Name)*

Given Name *(First Name)*   Full Middle Name

FOR INS USE ONLY

Bar Code   Date Stamp

Remarks

Action

Part 2. Information About Your Eligibility *(Check Only One)*

I am at least 18 years old **AND**

A. ☐ I have been a Lawful Permanent Resident of the United States for at least 5 years.

B. ☐ I have been a Lawful Permanent Resident of the United States for at least 3 years, AND I have been married to and living with the same U.S. citizen for the last 3 years, AND my spouse has been a U.S. citizen for the last 3 years.

C. ☐ I am applying on the basis of qualifying military service.

D. ☐ Other *(Please explain)* _____

Form N-400 (Rev. 05/31/01)N

Part 3. Information About You

A. Social Security Number

__ __ __ - __ __ - __ __ __ __

B. Date of Birth *(Month/Day/Year)*

__ __ / __ __ / __ __ __ __

C. Date You Became a Permanent Resident *(Month/Day/Year)*

__ __ / __ __ / __ __ __ __

D. Country of Birth

E. Country of Nationality

F. Are either of your parents U.S. citizens? *(if yes, see Instructions)* ☐ Yes ☐ No

G. What is your current marital status? ☐ Single, Never Married ☐ Married ☐ Divorced ☐ Widowed

☐ Marriage Annulled or Other *(Explain)* _____

H. Are you requesting a waiver of the English and/or U.S. History and Government requirements based on a disability or impairment and attaching a Form N-648 with your application? ☐ Yes ☐ No

I. Are you requesting an accommodation to the naturalization process because of a disability or impairment? *(See Instructions for some examples of accommodations.)* ☐ Yes ☐ No

If you answered "Yes", check the box below that applies:

☐ I am deaf or hearing impaired and need a sign language interpreter who uses the following language: _____

☐ I use a wheelchair.

☐ I am blind or sight impaired.

☐ I will need another type of accommodation. Please explain: _____

_____

_____

Part 4. Addresses and Telephone Numbers

A. Home Address - Street Number and Name *(Do NOT write a P.O. Box in this space)*   **Apartment Number**

City	County	State	ZIP Code	Country

B. Care of   **Mailing Address - Street Number and Name** *(If different from home address)*   **Apartment Number**

City	State	ZIP Code	Country

C. Daytime Phone Number *(If any)*   **Evening Phone Number** *(If any)*   **E-mail Address** *(If any)*

( )   ( )

Note: The categories below are those required by the FBI. See Instructions for more information.

A. Gender

☐ Male   ☐ Female

B. Height

| Feet | Inches |

C. Weight

| Pounds |

D. Race

☐ White   ☐ Asian or Pacific Islander   ☐ Black   ☐ American Indian or Alaskan Native   ☐ Unknown

E. Hair color

☐ Black   ☐ Brown   ☐ Blonde   ☐ Gray   ☐ White   ☐ Red   ☐ Sandy   ☐ Bald (No Hair)

F. Eye color

☐ Brown   ☐ Blue   ☐ Green   ☐ Hazel   ☐ Gray   ☐ Black   ☐ Pink   ☐ Maroon   ☐ Other

Part 6. Information About Your Residence and Employment

A. Where have you lived during the last 5 years? Begin with where you live now and then list every place you lived for the last 5 years. If you need more space, use a separate sheet of paper.

Street Number and Name, Apartment Number, City, State, Zip Code and Country	Dates (Month/Year) From	To
Current Home Address - Same as Part 4.A	_ _/_ _ _ _	Present
	_ _/_ _ _ _	_ _/_ _ _ _
	_ _/_ _ _ _	_ _/_ _ _ _
	_ _/_ _ _ _	_ _/_ _ _ _
	_ _/_ _ _ _	_ _/_ _ _ _

B. Where have you worked (or, if you were a student, what schools did you attend) during the last 5 years? Include military service. Begin with your current or latest employer and then list every place you have worked or studied for the last 5 years. If you need more space, use a separate sheet of paper.

Employer or School Name	Employer or School Address (Street, City and State)	Dates (Month/Year) From	To	Your Occupation
		_ _/_ _ _ _	_ _/_ _ _ _	
		_ _/_ _ _ _	_ _/_ _ _ _	
		_ _/_ _ _ _	_ _/_ _ _ _	
		_ _/_ _ _ _	_ _/_ _ _ _	
		_ _/_ _ _ _	_ _/_ _ _ _	

Part 7. Time Outside the United States
(Including Trips to Canada, Mexico, and the Caribbean Islands)

Write your INS "A"- number here:

A ___ ___ ___ ___ ___ ___ ___ ___ ___ ___

A. How many total days did you spend outside of the United States during the past 5 years?   [   ] days

B. How many trips of 24 hours or more have you taken outside of the United States during the past 5 years?   [   ] trips

C. List below all the trips of 24 hours or more that you have taken outside of the United States since becoming a Lawful Permanent Resident. Begin with your most recent trip. If you need more space, use a separate sheet of paper.

Date You Left the United States *(Month/Day/Year)*	Date You Returned to the United States *(Month/Day/Year)*	Did Trip Last 6 Months or More?	Countries to Which You Traveled	Total Days Out of the United States
___/___/___	___/___/___	☐ Yes ☐ No		
___/___/___	___/___/___	☐ Yes ☐ No		
___/___/___	___/___/___	☐ Yes ☐ No		
___/___/___	___/___/___	☐ Yes ☐ No		
___/___/___	___/___/___	☐ Yes ☐ No		
___/___/___	___/___/___	☐ Yes ☐ No		
___/___/___	___/___/___	☐ Yes ☐ No		
___/___/___	___/___/___	☐ Yes ☐ No		
___/___/___	___/___/___	☐ Yes ☐ No		
___/___/___	___/___/___	☐ Yes ☐ No		

Part 8. Information About Your Marital History

A. How many times have you been married (including annulled marriages)?   [   ]   If you have NEVER been married, go to Part 9.

B. If you are now married, give the following information about your spouse:

1. Spouse's Family Name *(Last Name)*   Given Name *(First Name)*   Full Middle Name *(If applicable)*

[   ]   [   ]   [   ]

2. Date of Birth *(Month/Day/Year)*   3. Date of Marriage *(Month/Day/Year)*   4. Spouse's Social Security Number

___/___/___   ___/___/___   ___ ___ ___ - ___ ___ - ___ ___ ___ ___

5. Home Address - Street Number and Name   Apartment Number

[   ]   [   ]

City   State   ZIP Code

[   ]   [   ]   [   ]

Write your INS "A"- number here:

A __ __ __ __ __ __ __ __ __

C. Is your spouse a U.S. citizen? ☐ Yes ☐ No

D. If your spouse is a U.S. citizen, give the following information:

1. When did your spouse become a U.S. citizen? ☐ At Birth ☐ Other

If "Other," give the following information:

2. Date your spouse became a U.S. citizen

____ / ____ / _____

3. Place your spouse became a U.S. citizen *(Please see Instructions)*

City and State

E. If your spouse is NOT a U.S. citizen, give the following information :

1. Spouse's Country of Citizenship

2. Spouse's INS "A"- Number *(If applicable)*

A ____ ____ ____ ____ ____ ____

3. Spouse's Immigration Status

☐ Lawful Permanent Resident   ☐ Other _____

F. If you were married before, provide the following information about your prior spouse. If you have more than one previous marriage, use a separate sheet of paper to provide the information requested in questions 1-5 below.

1. Prior Spouse's Family Name *(Last Name)*

Given Name *(First Name)*

Full Middle Name *(If applicable)*

2. Prior Spouse's Immigration Status

☐ U.S. Citizen

☐ Lawful Permanent Resident

☐ Other _____

3. Date of Marriage *(Month/Day/Year)*

____ / ____ / _____

4. Date Marriage Ended *(Month/Day/Year)*

____ / ____ / _____

5. How Marriage Ended

☐ Divorce   ☐ Spouse Died   ☐ Other _____

G. How many times has your current spouse been married (including annulled marriages)? ☐

If your spouse has EVER been married before, give the following information about your spouse's prior marriage.
If your spouse has more than one previous marriage, use a separate sheet of paper to provide the information requested in questions 1 - 5 below.

1. Prior Spouse's Family Name *(Last Name)*

Given Name *(First Name)*

Full Middle Name *(If applicable)*

2. Prior Spouse's Immigration Status

☐ U.S. Citizen

☐ Lawful Permanent Resident

☐ Other _____

3. Date of Marriage *(Month/Day/Year)*

____ / ____ / _____

4. Date Marriage Ended *(Month/Day/Year)*

____ / ____ / _____

5. How Marriage Ended

☐ Divorce   ☐ Spouse Died   ☐ Other _____

A. How many sons and daughters have you had? For more information on which sons and daughters you should include and how to complete this section, see the Instructions.

B. Provide the following information about all of your sons and daughters. If you need more space, use a separate sheet of paper.

Full Name of Son or Daughter	Date of Birth (Month/Day/Year)	INS "A"- number (if child has one)	Country of Birth	Current Address (Street, City, State & Country)
	_ _ / _ _ / _ _ _ _	A _ _ _ _ _ _ _ _ _		
	_ _ / _ _ / _ _ _ _	A _ _ _ _ _ _ _ _ _		
	_ _ / _ _ / _ _ _ _	A _ _ _ _ _ _ _ _ _		
	_ _ / _ _ / _ _ _ _	A _ _ _ _ _ _ _ _ _		
	_ _ / _ _ / _ _ _ _	A _ _ _ _ _ _ _ _ _		
	_ _ / _ _ / _ _ _ _	A _ _ _ _ _ _ _ _ _		
	_ _ / _ _ / _ _ _ _	A _ _ _ _ _ _ _ _ _		
	_ _ / _ _ / _ _ _ _	A _ _ _ _ _ _ _ _ _		

Part 10. Additional Questions

Please answer questions 1 through 14. If you answer "Yes" to any of these questions, include a written explanation with this form. Your written explanation should (1) explain why your answer was "Yes," and (2) provide any additional information that helps to explain your answer.

A. General Questions

1. Have you **EVER** claimed to be a U.S. citizen *(in writing or any other way)*? ☐ Yes ☐ No

2. Have you **EVER** registered to vote in any Federal, state, or local election in the United States? ☐ Yes ☐ No

3. Have you **EVER** voted in any Federal, state, or local election in the United States? ☐ Yes ☐ No

4. Since becoming a Lawful Permanent Resident, have you **EVER** failed to file a required Federal, state, or local tax return? ☐ Yes ☐ No

5. Do you owe any Federal, state, or local taxes that are overdue? ☐ Yes ☐ No

6. Do you have any title of nobility in any foreign country? ☐ Yes ☐ No

7. Have you ever been declared legally incompetent or been confined to a mental institution within the last 5 years? ☐ Yes ☐ No

B. Affiliations

8. a. Have you **EVER** been a member of or associated with any organization, association, fund, foundation, party, club, society, or similar group in the United States or in any other place?　☐ Yes　☐ No

b. If you answered "Yes," list the name of each group below. If you need more space, attach the names of the other group(s) on a separate sheet of paper.

Name of Group	Name of Group
1.	6.
2.	7.
3.	8.
4.	9.
5.	10.

9. Have you **EVER** been a member of or in any way associated *(either directly or indirectly)* with:

a. The Communist Party?　☐ Yes　☐ No

b. Any other totalitarian party?　☐ Yes　☐ No

c. A terrorist organization?　☐ Yes　☐ No

10. Have you **EVER** advocated *(either directly or indirectly)* the overthrow of any government by force or violence?　☐ Yes　☐ No

11. Have you **EVER** persecuted *(either directly or indirectly)* any person because of race, religion, national origin, membership in a particular social group, or political opinion?　☐ Yes　☐ No

12. Between March 23, 1933, and May 8, 1945, did you work for or associate in any way *(either directly or indirectly)* with:

a. The Nazi government of Germany?　☐ Yes　☐ No

b. Any government in any area (1) occupied by, (2) allied with, or (3) established with the help of the Nazi government of Germany?　☐ Yes　☐ No

c. Any German, Nazi, or S.S. military unit, paramilitary unit, self-defense unit, vigilante unit, citizen unit, police unit, government agency or office, extermination camp, concentration camp, prisoner of war camp, prison, labor camp, or transit camp?　☐ Yes　☐ No

C. Continuous Residence

Since becoming a Lawful Permanent Resident of the United States:

13. Have you **EVER** called yourself a "nonresident" on a Federal, state, or local tax return?　☐ Yes　☐ No

14. Have you **EVER** failed to file a Federal, state, or local tax return because you considered yourself to be a "nonresident"?　☐ Yes　☐ No

D. Good Moral Character

For the purposes of this application, you must answer "Yes" to the following questions, if applicable, even if your records were sealed or otherwise cleared or if anyone, including a judge, law enforcement officer, or attorney, told you that you no longer have a record.

15. Have you **EVER** committed a crime or offense for which you were NOT arrested?　　□ Yes　□ No

16. Have you **EVER** been arrested, cited, or detained by any law enforcement officer (including INS and military officers) for any reason?　　□ Yes　□ No

17. Have you **EVER** been charged with committing any crime or offense?　　□ Yes　□ No

18. Have you **EVER** been convicted of a crime or offense?　　□ Yes　□ No

19. Have you **EVER** been placed in an alternative sentencing or a rehabilitative program (for example: diversion, deferred prosecution, withheld adjudication, deferred adjudication)?　　□ Yes　□ No

20. Have you **EVER** received a suspended sentence, been placed on probation, or been paroled?　　□ Yes　□ No

21. Have you **EVER** been in jail or prison?　　□ Yes　□ No

If you answered "Yes" to any of questions 15 through 21, complete the following table. If you need more space, use a separate sheet of paper to give the same information.

Why were you arrested, cited, detained, or charged?	Date arrested, cited, detained, or charged *(Month/Day/Year)*	Where were you arrested, cited, detained or charged? *(City, State, Country)*	Outcome or disposition of the arrest, citation, detention or charge *(No charges filed, charges dismissed, jail, probation, etc.)*

Answer questions 22 through 33. If you answer "Yes" to any of these questions, attach (1) your written explanation why your answer was "Yes," and (2) any additional information or documentation that helps explain your answer.

22. Have you **EVER**:

　a. been a habitual drunkard?　　□ Yes　□ No

　b. been a prostitute, or procured anyone for prostitution?　　□ Yes　□ No

　c. sold or smuggled controlled substances, illegal drugs or narcotics?　　□ Yes　□ No

　d. been married to more than one person at the same time?　　□ Yes　□ No

　e. helped anyone enter or try to enter the United States illegally?　　□ Yes　□ No

　f. gambled illegally or received income from illegal gambling?　　□ Yes　□ No

　g. failed to support your dependents or to pay alimony?　　□ Yes　□ No

23. Have you **EVER** given false or misleading information to any U.S. government official while applying for any immigration benefit or to prevent deportation, exclusion, or removal?　　□ Yes　□ No

24. Have you **EVER** lied to any U.S. government official to gain entry or admission into the United States?　　□ Yes　□ No

E. Removal, Exclusion, and Deportation Proceedings

25. Are removal, exclusion, rescission or deportation proceedings pending against you? ☐Yes ☐No

26. Have you **EVER** been removed, excluded, or deported from the United States? ☐Yes ☐No

27. Have you **EVER** been ordered to be removed, excluded, or deported from the United States? ☐Yes ☐No

28. Have you **EVER** applied for any kind of relief from removal, exclusion, or deportation? ☐Yes ☐No

F. Military Service

29. Have you **EVER** served in the U.S. Armed Forces? ☐Yes ☐No

30. Have you **EVER** left the United States to avoid being drafted into the U.S. Armed Forces? ☐Yes ☐No

31. Have you **EVER** applied for any kind of exemption from military service in the U.S. Armed Forces? ☐Yes ☐No

32. Have you **EVER** deserted from the U.S. Armed Forces? ☐Yes ☐No

G. Selective Service Registration

33. Are you a male who lived in the United States at any time between your 18th and 26th birthdays in any status except as a lawful nonimmigrant? ☐Yes ☐No

If you answered "NO", go on to question 34.

If you answered "YES", provide the information below.

If you answered "YES", but you did NOT register with the Selective Service System and are still under 26 years of age, you must register before you apply for naturalization, so that you can complete the information below:

Date Registered (Month/Day/Year) [   ]   Selective Service Number [_ _ / _ _ _ / _ _ _ _]

If you answered "YES", but you did NOT register with the Selective Service and you are now 26 years old or older, attach a statement explaining why you did not register.

H. Oath Requirements *(See Part 14 for the text of the oath)*

Answer questions 34 through 39. If you answer "No" to any of these questions, attach (1) your written explanation why the answer was "No" and (2) any additional information or documentation that helps to explain your answer.

34. Do you support the Constitution and form of government of the United States? ☐Yes ☐No

35. Do you understand the full Oath of Allegiance to the United States? ☐Yes ☐No

36. Are you willing to take the full Oath of Allegiance to the United States? ☐Yes ☐No

37. If the law requires it, are you willing to bear arms on behalf of the United States? ☐Yes ☐No

38. If the law requires it, are you willing to perform noncombatant services in the U.S. Armed Forces? ☐Yes ☐No

39. If the law requires it, are you willing to perform work of national importance under civilian direction? ☐Yes ☐No

Part 11. Your Signature

Write your INS "A"- number here:

A _ _ _ _ _ _ _ _ _

I certify, under penalty of perjury under the laws of the United States of America, that this application, and the evidence submitted with it, are all true and correct. I authorize the release of any information which INS needs to determine my eligibility for naturalization.

Your Signature

Date *(Month/Day/Year)*

_ _ / _ _ / _ _ _ _

Part 12. Signature of Person Who Prepared This Application for You *(if applicable)*

I declare under penalty of perjury that I prepared this application at the request of the above person. The answers provided are based on information of which I have personal knowledge and/or were provided to me by the above named person in response to the *exact questions* contained on this form.

Preparer's Printed Name

Preparer's Signature

Date *(Month/Day/Year)*

_ _ / _ _ / _ _ _ _

Preparer's Firm or Organization Name *(If applicable)*

Preparer's Daytime Phone Number

( )

Preparer's Address - Street Number and Name

City

State

ZIP Code

Do Not Complete Parts 13 and 14 Until an INS Officer Instructs You To Do So

Part 13. Signature at Interview

I swear (affirm) and certify under penalty of perjury under the laws of the United States of America that I know that the contents of this application for naturalization subscribed by me, including corrections numbered 1 through _____ and the evidence submitted by me numbered pages 1 through _____, are true and correct to the best of my knowledge and belief.

Subscribed to and sworn to (affirmed) before me

Officer's Printed Name or Stamp

Date *(Month/Day/Year)*

Complete Signature of Applicant

Officer's Signature

Part 14. Oath of Allegiance

If your application is approved, you will be scheduled for a public oath ceremony at which time you will be required to take the following oath of allegiance immediately prior to becoming a naturalized citizen. By signing below, you acknowledge your willingness and ability to take this oath:

I hereby declare, on oath, that I absolutely and entirely renounce and abjure all allegiance and fidelity to any foreign prince, potentate, state, or sovereignty, of whom or which which I have heretofore been a subject or citizen;

that I will support and defend the Constitution and laws of the United States of America against all enemies, foreign and domestic;
that I will bear true faith and allegiance to the same;
that I will bear arms on behalf of the United States when required by the law;
that I will perform noncombatant service in the Armed Forces of the United States when required by the law;
that I will perform work of national importance under civilian direction when required by the law; and
that I take this obligation freely, without any mental reservation or purpose of evasion; so help me God.

Printed Name of Applicant

Complete Signature of Applicant